REPORT AND EVIDENCE

OF THE

COMMITTEE ON ARBITRARY ARRESTS,

IN THE

STATE OF INDIANA,

AUTHORIZED BY RESOLUTION OF THE HOUSE OF REPRESENTATIVES, JANUARY 9, 1863.

FIVE THOUSAND COPIES ORDERED TO BE PRINTED.

INDIANAPOLIS:
JOSEPH J. BINGHAM, STATE PRINTER.
1863.

ARBITRARY ARRESTS IN INDIANA.

EVIDENCE ACCOMPANYING THE REPORT OF THE HOUSE COMMITTEE OF THE GENERAL ASSEMBLY ON ARBITRARY ARRESTS IN THE STATE OF INDIANA.

HOUSE OF REPRESENTATIVES,
January 9, 1863.

On motion of the Hon. Jason B. Brown, of Jackson county, the following resolutions were adopted:

WHEREAS, The Constitution of the United States and of the State of Indiana solemnly guarantee to the people thereof freedom of speech, freedom of the press, the sacred right of the writ of habeas corpus, security from arrest without due process of law, and that in all criminal prosecutions the accused shall enjoy the right to a speedy and public trial by an impartial jury of the State and district wherein the crime shall have been committed, and to be informed of the nature and cause of the accusation, to be confronted with the witnesses against him, and have compulsory process for obtaining witnesses, counsel, &c.; and,

WHEREAS, We have witnessed, within the past twenty months, the violation of all these provisions so indispensable to a free government and necessary for the enjoyment of public liberty, by means alike arbitrary, violent, insulting, and degrading to a degree unknown to any government on earth, except those avowedly and notoriously wicked, cruel, and despotic; and,

WHEREAS, We, the Representatives of the people, now assembled in a legislative capacity, charged with the high duty of enacting laws for the protection of the people and the preservation of their rights, deem it our first duty to ascertain the facts connected with the criminal usurpations and wrongs which have been practiced by political arrests, and in order to give those who have unlawfully made them, or caused them to be made, the prominence to a position of lasting infamy their conduct merits, alike as punishment and as a warning to others hereafter, and to enable us to act intelligently and efficiently in providing such legislation as will prevent their repetition, therefore,

Resolved, That a committee of seven be appointed by this House, whose duty it shall be to report to this body the number of arrests for political causes made within the limits of the State, and all the facts connected with each, showing by whose order, procurement or influence, either immediate or remote, the arrests were made, the place, time, and manner of the same, and by whom made; the charges (if any) made against them, and the probability of their truth or falsity; the place and duration of their imprisonment, and their treatment; the trial, or opportunity for trial, which they may have had, if any; the circumstances of their discharge, if discharged; the injury to their persons or families (if any) which have resulted from their unlawful detention, and the damages or pecuniary loss sustained by them in consequence of their imprisonment.

Resolved, That said committee also inquire into and report if there have been obstructions to the free exercise of the liberty of speech or press, or any abridgement thereof within the past two years in this State, and, if so, report the facts connected therewith.

Resolved, That said committee be authorized to report a bill that shall contain provisions adequate to protect the people from the arbitrary commission of unconstitutional acts, by such penalties and punishment upon those guilty of the same as may effectually prevent their repetition, and provide means for redress and restitution by damages or otherwise to requite their wrongs, while serving as an exemplary warning to other usurpers in all time to come.

Resolved, That said committee be and are hereby authorized and empowered to send for persons and papers, or visit any locality within the State, that may be deemed necessary to the full and complete discharge of their duty.

In pursuance of the above resolutions, the Speaker appointed the following committee:

Hon.	Jason B. Brown,	of	Jackson	County.
"	Bayless W. Hanna,	"	Vigo	"
"	O. S. Given,	"	Daviess	"
"	Jonas G. Howard,	"	Clark	"
"	Edwin P. Ferris,	"	Ripley	"
"	Chas. B. Laselle,	"	Cass	"
"	Samuel A. Shoaf,	"	Jay	"
"	Benj. F. Gregory,	"	Warren	"
"	James M. Gregg,	"	Hendricks	"
"	Chas. D. Morgan,	"	Henry	"
"	Timothy Baker,	"	Noble	"

Committee Room, January 23, 1863.

The Committee assembled at their room, and organized by appointing Ethelbert C. Hibben, of Rush county, Secretary of said Committee.

The Committee on Arbitrary Arrests, after hearing and examining the evidence submitted to them under the resolutions of the House, beg leave to submit the following report:

REPORT

OF

THE COMMITTEE.

Under the resolution of the House we have examined witnesses in forty-three cases of arrests made in our State, and accompanying this is the evidence laid before us in those cases.

Several matters suggest themselves to our minds in connection with the facts thus developed—matters which, in the judgment of the Committee, deeply affect the liberty and vital welfare of the people of Indiana. Acts have been perpetrated, and omissions of duty suffered by high officers, which, if left unnoticed and unrebuked, would exhibit to the world a shameless want of fidelity on the part of the representatives of the people toward their constituents, and if such lack of fidelity should be sanctioned, it would go far toward establishing that which appears to be assumed as true, by those who have for two years controled affairs, namely, that the people have ceased to take an interest in the mode and manner in which the government ought to be administered. In short, that it is no longer a government of the people, through their agents, the chosen officers of the law—but a government in which the servant has become the master, and the superior the slave.

The tendency of the legislation and acts of those placed in power by the people for the last two years, has been to curtail the liberties and to crush the spirit of independence of those who have placed them in position. The many acts of arbitrary power shown by this evidence, taken in connection with the attempt by the Congress and President of the United States, to shield from all responsibility, those who in the very wantonness of power have been guilty of such unwarranted acts, make a dark chapter in the mournful history which is to be written of the demoralization of the public men, and the downward tendency of the public morals of the times.

It must be a truth that if our sires refused to submit to the wanton acts of the minions of a king, who was the descendant of a long line of rulers, whom they and their ancestors had been educated to respect, obey, and reverence, that public virtue must have greatly declined, yea, that it is almost extinct, if we, their sons, will quietly crouch down to receive the lash, and hold out our hands for the fetters with which the lowest subordinates of a public servant would degrade us—for the President of the United States, by its Constitution, is but the servant of the sovereign people.

Has it indeed come to this, that we must speak of our public servants with bated breath, and that we must approach with unsandled feet when we would come into their presence to seek a redress of wrongs? Are the laws of nature to be reversed, and has the mere creature become greater than the creator? Can we no longer set forth our grievances, either real or fancied, as our fathers did, in the immortal declaration of their independence?

The arrests that have been investigated by the Committee may be resolved into four classes:—

Second. For treasonable practices.
First. For obstructing the draft.
Third. For disloyal practices.
Fourth. For no cause at all.

In point of fact, it will be seen by every intelligent, candid person, who may take the pains to read this evidence, and who will read it with a desire to arrive at the truth, that nine out of every ten of those who were arrested fell under the head of the fourth class, and the remainder were taken into custody upon frivolous pretexts that could have been dissipated in a very short explanation before any intelligent, unprejudiced tribunal, if permission had been granted to that end. Indeed, it is scarcely necessary to offer arguments to show this fact, since those in power have conceded the whole question, by discharging nearly all the parties arrested, without even the semblance of a hearing or trial. In but few instances were such discharges made, until the victims of misapplied power had suffered great inconvenience, expense, and in many cases loss of health. The utter falsity of the pretended reasons for arrests were thus admitted, and the innocence of the sufferers reluctantly declared by their persecutors.

The great and controling motive of those who have resorted to such an arbitrary course toward the people, appears to have been a desire to prevent investigation into their acts, in the first instance; so that if the people would patiently endure it, they might go on gradually encroaching upon their simplicity in the exercise of unauthorized acts, until they should not be even shocked at the assumption of absolute and supreme power, if in the end it should be thought necessary by those in office for the attainment of their ultimate purposes. If this is not the correct reason for the acts complained of, we can see no cause for the arrests being confined to one political party alone. Many of these arrests, indeed nearly all of them, were made before the Administration had progressed to the length desired by the ultra Abolitionists; and because of the apparently conservative tendencies of Mr. Lincoln in the earlier periods of his term of office, he and his policy had been more bitterly opposed and denounced by members of the Abolition party, than by those Democrats who were arrested. No Abolitionist who thus indulged in denunciations of the policy of the conduct of the war was arrested, but the least offense in that respect by a Democrat was met by the stern hand of power. Why was this? Two reasons present themselves: First, without doubt it was the intention of Mr. Lincoln, from the beginning of the war, gradually but ultimately, to lead it on to the purposes of emancipation; and he would thus, at the proper time, fall into the arms of the Abolitionists—therefore, it would not do to offend and alienate them in advance. Secondly, the history of Democracy shows that they have always been in favor of the greatest freedom of opinion, and of granting the largest measures of personal liberty to the individual members of society. The course marked out would not admit of the expression, or even possession of this kind of liberty. It is, and always has been, in antagonism to arbitrary power. For hundreds of years, a war has been going on between this Democratic principle of individual liberty, and its opposite, the concentration of such liberty in the hands of a few only, at the expense of the many. To be free thus to seize the reins of power unlawfully, it became necessary to silence men who had been educated in this school of freedom and equality. Those who spoke boldly, as freemen ought to do, were seized, deprived of liberty, and refused a trial, under the pretext that they had been guilty of disloyal practices; not with the expectation of convicting them, but with the hope that such acts would deter others from canvassing with like freedom the acts of usurpation of those in authority.

In carefully considering this testimony, the Committee can not avoid the conclusion, that the acts thereby shown, clearly demonstrate a kind of morbid fear of the *people* upon the part of the *rulers.* They appear to apprehend that the course being pursued does not meet with public approbation. For instance, a word said against the President, or his mode of managing affairs, in the alarm of subordinates, is by them construed to be a disloyal practice, and the offender, if a Democrat, is immediately arrested and put where he can do no more harm.

In England, we believe, they once had a statute declaring it treason of a certain grade for a man to "imagine the death of the king," and one subject was convicted under this statute for wishing the king had a buck's horns in his belly, on the ground that he could not have had them there and lived, consequently the man must have wished for his death. We laugh at the folly of such a law, when the question is put directly to us, and yet for many months we have been submitting to a vague and unsettled proclamation in regard to disloyal practices, as construed by young, ambitious adventurers, strutting their brief hour upon the stage, without identity and without responsibility. We are indeed a patient people—of long forbearance—full of brotherly love, and overflowing with the milk of human kindness. In the opinion of one A. B. Jetmore, who resides in Hartford City, Blackford county, who states, on his oath, that he is a lawyer, it is a "great crime and burning shame for any one to speak or argue against the views or policy of the National Executive." How precipitant and how deep is the descent, in the scale of law and in the doctrines of political liberty, from Mansfield and Blackstone, Marshall and Taney, Blackford and Dewey, to Abraham B. Jetmore, Esq. He says he used to be a Democrat. Poor fellow! he is now a convicted spy upon his neighbors, who have put bread into his mouth, and clothes upon his back. Doubtless he has already received his little price. The Committee would recommend him to the clemency of the latter-day Abraham, whom he considers so far superior to all laws, institutions, and constitutions, whether civil or divine.

CASE OF JUDGE CONSTABLE.

But leaving these questions, we propose to look more in detail at the classes of cases presented; but before doing so, we desire to call special attention to the case of Judge Constable. He is not a resident of Indiana, but he was brought into the State and imprisoned here. We do this for the reason that the principle involved in his case is closely connected with civil liberty itself. What is it that distinguishes civilization from barbarism? The one is established upon conditional rules—wise, humane, determinate laws; the other is the sudden growth of prejudice, selfishness, and passion, affording shelter to-day and bringing swift destruction to-morrow. Upon the just administration of the conventional rules and prescribed laws upon which civilization is built, depends its highest degree of perfection. All writers agree that to insure this end magistrates of the law should be learned, independent, unbiased, and honest; and thus qualified, they must be left to act freely. No man could thus act if, for an honest error of judgment, he should be subjected to penalties. Every beginner in the study of law knows this. And why is it? Because of the fallibility of the human mind. No man is infallible. A judge must decide one way or another upon questions presented to him. He has no choice as to that. He may decide wrong. Superior courts are instituted to correct his decisions if he does. The imprisonment, or even worse punishment of the judge, would not reverse that judgment. And further, no honest, upright man would, for a moment, hold a judicial office with the possibility of penalties, either civil or criminal, attaching to an error of judgment. For these, among other reasons, it is a settled and known principle of legal jurisprudence, that a magistrate or judge can not be made to respond, either criminally or in damages, in a civil suit, because of any official decision he may honestly make. This is to support his dignity and authority, and to draw veneration to his person, and submission to his judgment. In support of this theory, the committee would refer to the following standard English and American authorities: Co. Litt. 294; 2 Just. 422; 2 Dall. R. 160; 1 Yeates' R. 443; 2 N. & McC. 168; 1 Day. R. 315; 1 Root R. 211; 3 Caines' R. 170; 5 John. R. 282; 9 John. R. 395; 11 John. R. 150; 3 Marsh. R. 76; 1 South. R. 74; 1 N. H. Rep. 374; 2 Bay. 1, 69; 8 Wend. 468; 3 Marsh R. 76.

If it were otherwise, judges would be the mere tools of those in authority, there would be no independence of thought or action. No citizen could safely trust his interests in the keeping, or to the determination of a judiciary thus trammeled. Communities would be driven back toward a state of barbarism. Every man would be compelled to take into his own hands the adjudication of his own controversies. The strong would govern the weak. Men would combine together in clans and factions to protect each other. This condition of things would be anarchy.

In the above suggestions we have assumed that Judge Constable committed an error in the judicial decision upon which he was arrested—but in fact he did not, as could be amply shown, if it was at all necessary to enter into an argument on the subject. But it is not necessary, for, conceding for the sake of the argument that he was in error in his decision, it is not pretended that he decided corruptly, and therefore, all the reasons we have stated, fully apply in favor of the freedom and independence of the judiciary in his case. Again, admitting he was wrong, in England even, from whose oppressions we separated by a long war, it is held by the king, that "he looks upon the independence and uprightness of the judges as essential to the impartial administration of justice—as one of the best securities of the *rights and liberties of his subjects*, and as most conducive to the honor of the crown." Ld. Raym. 747, Blkst. Com., Jacob's L. Dict., 3, 547.

A judge is not answerable then, even to the king, for an error of judgment in a matter of which he has jurisdiction. 1 Salk. 397, 2 Hawk., c. 1, sec. 17.

But here, the President, as Commander-in-Chief, through his subordinates, usurps greater powers than the king in England dare exercise, for through them he undertakes to determine when a judge has decided right or wrong, and to punish him for that decision—not by any regular course of judicial proceeding, either civil or criminal, nor yet by the mode pointed out by the Constitution for corrupt acts, which is by impeachment, but by an arbitrary Turkish process of military despotism, merely because, as in the case of Mr. Green, these gentlemen may believe they are "backed by six hundred thousand bayonets."

It is time that the people should arouse to a just sense of the great danger to their liberties, when the men and the money they have placed at the disposal of the Government are thus boastingly diverted from the purpose for which they were furnished.

BLACKFORD COUNTY CASES.

The Committee, in treating of the evidence as it has been developed, and according to the classification of offenses, would invite attention, first, to the Blackford County cases, where eighteen arrests were made, as declared by the authorities, for resistance to the draft. These arrests will astonish everybody—a tyrant would be ashamed of them. Without the semblance of guilt, without a shadow of pretext, in the absence of all reason, forgetting all reverence for law and personal liberty, a few weak and misguided creatures, calling themselves the officers of the law, in the night-time, and acting under false pretenses, seize and carry away from their families and homes unoffending and peaceable citizens—citizens of character, of inflnence, and position; and after they are thus seized and dragged away, these irresponsible wretches hunt an occasion to appease their wicked and gangrened party malevolence, by exposing these kidnapped prisoners, in the streets at Indianapolis, to the jeers and derision of a remorseless mob. They are cast into prison, and there, within the damp walls of their dungeon cells, without comfortable bedding, fed upon tainted food, they are left to become the prey of disease and the victims of death.

Thus outraged and thus fettered, they call upon their accusers to come forth and confront them. The officers having them in charge are asked of what crimes they are accused—an examination by some legally constituted tribunal is repeatedly demanded. They had a right thus to be brought into the presence of their accusers; they had a right to demand the reasons of their restraint; it is an ancient and well established right—a right guaranteed by the Constitution of the United States, and the Constitution of the State of Indiana; but their appeals were addressed to the hard hearts and deaf ears of tyrants.

The United States Marshal, when appealed to, folds himself more warmly in the flowing cloak of his own luxury, and with a view to shift the responsibility, he wags his head ominously, and points these outraged citizens to the modern Caligula and his willing satraps, who now inhabit the ancient metropolis of Republican liberty:—There, he says, is my authority; I must obey—ask me nothing more.

But all this does not satisfy the people, who are jealous of their liberties. They will not be put off. Our rights and liberties are common rights and liberties. That which wrongs a citizen, wrongs the State. There stands the stubborn question, How were these arrests made? The prisoners are told upon affidavit. Upon whose affidavit? Who can tell? Some one is responsible, certainly! We have laws, we have courts, we have a Governor for our protection, and he is the sworn custodian of our peace and liberties. How does it come to pass that all these great elements of power and protection were powerless and silent in this great emergency? The people of this country are free, unless placed under restraint for the violation of some law, and then only by positive proof, with the presumption of innocence in their favor until proved guilty. Here citizens of Indiana were restrained of their liberty, and denied a trial. Why did not the Executive, made so by the Constitution, and backed as such by the whole military power of the State, enforce the constitutional and unquestioned rights of these citizens? Was he ignorant of the fact that they had been trampled upon? That could not be. He does not pretend so much. One million of free Americans, of Anglo-Saxon-Celtic descent, ask the question—Where was he while these monstrous outrages were being practiced upon the liberties of the great people whose fortunes and destiny were the especial objects of his care? Was he in league with the oppressor? or was he only sleeping, like Anthony, folded in the voluptuous arms of some Cleopatra, while the safety of the city, and the liberties of the citizen, were left exposed to the clemency of the vandal and the knife of the assassin? There is a serious question couched in all this outrage, which, sooner or later, Governor Morton will be called upon to answer. The people, who have suffered so severely, will neither forget or forgive these unparalleled and wicked wrongs.

The Committee have looked in vain in all the cases for the pretext upon which the arrests were made. The story out of doors is, they were made in vindication of the destruction of the draft-box in Hartford City, which it is said was done on the 6th day of October, 1862.

Upon careful investigation, the Committee have ascertained that the draft-box was destroyed there at that time by one Jesse Williams, who was drunk at the time, and who has not to this day been arrested for it. The evidence shows clearly that Williams is the only man who had any thing to do with the destruction of the draft-box: still Andrew Brickley, Frank Taughinbaugh, Elihu Lyon, William Armstrong, Thomas Daugherty, John M. Vanhorn,

John McManamon, Dr. William Schull, Leander Tarr, Thomas Longfellow, Daniel Watson, Jacob Clapper, John Miller, Henry Snyder and Bluford Mills, all Democrats, are seized by the authorities, and without warrant are cast into prison, and without mittimus are held there by the United States Marshal—some for several days—others for weeks—and then discharged and sent home without a trial. Bluford Mills lost his life in this wicked affair—upon those who have been instrumental in taking the life of a valuable and intelligent citizen rests this terrible guilt. Anguish of soul will overtake them some time on account of it. If not before, they will feel it at last in that dark and melancholy hour, when with feeble breath, they shall come to falter forth their last cry for mercy on an erring life.

Andrew Brickley, one of the parties arrested, is the sheriff of Blackford county—a gentleman of the highest standing in the community where he resides—as an evidence of his respectability and standing, he has received the indorsement of a majority of the people of the county where he lives. He, among others of the highest respectability, is arrested, and what is the evidence against him—nothing—not a word—on the contrary, he had used his influence to allay the excitement at Hartford City, where the draft was to be made. It is true he had agreed to assist in the work of the draft, he had agreed to do so for the satisfaction of his neighbors, who had faith in his integrity, and who believed he would protect them from fraud and party partiality. He proposed to act according to his understanding of the orders issued from the War Department, at Washington. But no, Mr. Frash had received special instructions from Governor Morton which must not be departed from. Governor Morton, in his ambition to dispense patronage, could not rest satisfied with the orders at Washington. Notwithstanding the people were already suspicious of his public integrity, and notwithstanding a large majority of them believed he would draft Democrats to the fullest extent that his slavish tools dared to venture—notwithstanding numerous complaints had been made to that effect in all parts of the State, still the Indianapolis programme must be carried out. So, Frash, the pliant tool of this no-party Governor, was allowed to have his own way, and Mr. Brickley, for allowing him this contested privelege, in the opinion of these gentlemen, became a great criminal, and was thrown into jail for it.

Not one witness examined, says that any one of those who were imprisoned, in any way aided or abetted in the destruction of the draft-box. Poor Allen Ward did so testify, but he afterward said that his statement was false. Let this testimony show for itself—here it is in full:—

Mr. Morgan.—" Who did you see engaged in stamping on the box?"

Mr. Ward.—" I saw Jesse Williams, Andrew Williams, John Dougherty, Thomas Dougherty, John Vanhorn and Bluford Mills."

Mr. Morgan.—" Who did you see hallooing, cheering, and stamping on the floor?"

Mr. Ward.—" Besides these I have named, I saw Leander Tarr, Daniel Watson, Henry Lyons, John Miller, Henry Snyder, and John P. Garr."

Mr. Ferris.—" What is your politics?"

Mr. Ward.—" I am a Republican."

Mr. Ferris.—" How many men were there in the Court House when the draft-box was mashed?"

Mr. Ward.—" About a hundred."

Mr. Ferris.—" Do you swear positively that Jesse Williams, John and Thomas Dougherty, John Vanhorn and Bluford Mills, were each of them engaged in stamping the box and throwing the pieces around?"

Mr. Ward.—" Yes sir."

Mr. Ferris.—" How much was the box broken, into how many pieces?"

Mr. Ward.—" The rim was broken into two pieces, and each head into the same number of pieces."

Mr. Ferris.—" Who did you see throwing the pieces around?"

Mr. Ward..—" I can not name any person."

Mr. Ferris.—" Name the persons you know you saw stamping the box."

Mr. Ward.—" I saw Jess. Williams. He is the only one I can swear I saw stamping the box."

Mr. Ferris.—" If you stated that any person except Williams stamped on the box, or the pieces, was that true?"

Mr. Ward.—" To be certain, Jess. Williams was the only person I saw stamping the box to pieces."

Mr. Ferris.—" Could you have heard it had any one hurrahed for Jeff. Davis before the crowd left the Court House?"

Mr. Ward.—" Yes, I could."

Mr. Ferris.—" Was there any hallooing for Jeff. Davis in the house?"

Mr. Ward.—"If there was I did not hear it."

Mr. Ferris.—"If you swore that any of the six men you named, besides Williams, was engaged in throwing around the pieces of the box, was that statement true?"

Mr. Ward.—"I saw none but Williams have hold of the box, or any of the pieces."

Mr. Ferris.—"If you stated that Leander Tarr, Daniel Watson, Henry Snyder, John P. Garr, and John Miller were there hallooing, was that statement true?"

Mr. Ward.—"I can not be positive that every one of them was."

Mr. Ferris—"Was there any stamping done in the room that you know of, except that done on the box?"

Mr. Ward.—"None that I could name."

Mr. Ferris.—"Now if you stated that any person except Williams was engaged in stamping on the floor, was that statement true?"

Mr. Ward.—"I saw John Dougherty and Bluford Mills jumping up and down on the floor."

The Committee have recited this testimony in full, that the public may be forcibly impressed with the utter futility of the claims upon which these arrests were made. William Frash, Christopher Clapper, Dwight Klinck, James Crosby, Abraham Stahl, and Allen Ward were summoned by Republican members of this Committee, to relieve, if possible, the parties who made the Blackford county arrests of actual disgrace and crime. How far they have succeeded the public must judge from the testimony. The Committee forbear to enter further into this discussion, the whole case is fully presented to the public, all may read it and digest it for themselves. There will certainly be an end to this kind of oppression—when the oppressor, shorn of patronage, and unsupported by the willing slaves of place and emolument, will once more stand upon his own footing, and thus reduced to the true condition of responsibility, he will be constrained to render up an account that will be satisfactory to the inexorable citizen who has been so wantonly and so wickedly outraged.

TREASONABLE PRACTICES.

Under this head may be classed what is familiarly known as the Newburg cases, together with the arrest of W. B. McLean, of Vanderburg county.

As to the Newburg cases it is a notorious fact, and it is a part of the recent history of this State, that in these arrests an attempt was made to defeat the Democratic party in the last October elections. It was proclaimed by the leading republican organ of the State, that one of the Newburg prisoners had drafted resolutions—another had done this, and another that in the county convention assembled in Warrick county, to indorse the action of the 8th of January convention. And therefore it was contended by these insignificant philosophers, that the people ought not to trust a party made up of such disloyal members. After all this parade and flourish of trumpets, it would have been too bare-faced to have turned loose the parties arrested, without some show of a trial. Therefore, in the United States Court a grand jury was gotten up for the occasion, controlled, as everybody knows it was, by a number of ancient and hacknied party fossils, appointed by partizans, to work up to a partizan programme, which they did without stint or conscience. The Committee are advised there are some honorable exceptions in this grand jury, who positively refused to debase themselves. But that the people of the State may be fully apprized as to who the guilty parties are, that have published what they had no right to publish, and what they could only publish by a positive violation of their oath, their names are given to the world. The old maxim of law, false in one thing false in all things, raises a very serious question between the honest people and the unscrupulous members of this grand jury. Here they are:—

William P. Fishback,
Charles H. Test,
George Moon,
William A. Montgomery,
James Blake,
T. B. McCarty,
Daniel Sigler,
Leonidas Sexton,
Benjamin G. Stout,
James Hill,
Daniel Sagre,
H. D. Scott,
Robert Parrett, and
Fred. S. Brown.

When they were impanneled, they *swore* to keep secret all their proceedings; but they had not been in session a single week, until members of this same grand jury, and other persons in their confidence, were making speeches all over the State—adjourning their meetings for that purpose—retailing what the jury in secret session, clothed in the habiliments of abandoned and remorseless party camp followers, and not acting within the true intent and meaning of their solemn obligations as jurors, had discovered, as they supposed in their willing spirit, to be treasonable practices on the part of the Democratic party throughout this State. Of course all these reports were false in fact, or else these partizan jurors were false to their oaths. Let them elect which horn of the dilemma they will take. But the inquisition had been established—the blocks for the execution had been placed there—they must be stained with blood—the executioner was impatient for the work of death; indictments were found, and the United States Attorney, in pursuance of his undoubted right, selected the strongest case from the Newburg prisoners, and with all the aid of the marshal in the selection of a traverse jury, he failed to convict his chosen victim of the offense charged, and indeed of any offense. And so the matter stands—it has become a part of the history of the people of Indiana—a source of humiliation and disgrace, and attainder to all the parties who have thus prostituted themselves for the subservience of selfish and malevolent party schemes. This is about the last we will hear of Newburg treasonable practices. The evidence is given to the public in full; it will be weighed carefully; and at some period in the future, not far distant, we will have the popular verdict upon it. The boys in the streets will yet mock at the members of this grand jury, who have so disgraced themselves; and their children after them will spend a lifetime of mortification on account of the ignominy that has been entailed upon them.

In this connection the Committee would invite attention to the case of W. B. McLean, a citizen of Evansville, Indiana. It is an uninviting picture. Mr. McLean was induced to go to Indianapolis by General Blythe, in consideration of vague rumors circulating against his loyalty, that he might answer to Governor Morton; and if by him, or his military tribunal, acquitted, the suggestion was that all excitement against him would be subdued. He was promised an immediate hearing. General Blythe was in command of the military forces in southwestern Indiana, and Mr. McLean supposed that he would perform his promises, that upon his arrival at Indianapolis he would have a hearing, and he knew he would be acquitted, for he was guilty of no crime. But how was he treated? He was cast into this mighty whirlpool of frenzy, and left for weeks at the mercy of half-fledged officials, who either did not know their duty, or if they did, who were too unscrupulous to perform it. General Blythe knew that Mr. McLean had a wife and five helpless children dependent upon his daily labor for support; but no, that mattered nothing. Party favorites must be gratified by his humiliation. And what did it all amount to? nothing. He had sent a pistol to a cousin in Kentucky, *with the written permit of A. T. Robinson, the surveyor of the port at Evansville.* This is all that it was pretended he had done, for which he was kept in close confinement for more than six weeks. Shame upon a Government that would commit such crime against the liberty of the unoffending citizen, simply because it had the physical power to do so. But it was done—it can not be denied—it is not denied. Let the responsibility rest where it belongs.

DISLOYAL PRACTICES.

This appears to be a cant phrase of Greeley coinage, and means any thing or nothing; the Committee are unable to determine which. In its popular acceptation, it seems to signify Democratic theories and ideas as opposed to Republican theories and ideas. It is, perhaps, nothing more than a term of reproach. But classing it as an offense, according to the construction of Abolitionists, the Committee would call attention to two or three of the most prominent cases which have been developed under it.

It will not be necessary to enter very far into details, as the evidence will only have to be read to be clearly understood. Especial attention is invited to the arrests of Harris Reynolds, of Fountain county, Dr. Theodore Horton, of Wells county, Richard Slater, of Dearborn county, and Amos Green, a citizen of the State of Illinois, who was arrested in Terre Haute. These gentlemen were arrested near about the same time, and very nearly for similar reasons. Harris Reynolds was arrested upon a false charge of having advised resistance to the draft, on the first day of October, 1862, and was discharged without trial on the 22d day of the same month. Dr. Theodore Horton, arrested on the 9th day of October, 1862, for making a speech in favor of a strict construction of the Constitution of the United States, was confined in the prison at Indianapolis until the 13th day of November, and was then discharged by Mr. Rose without trial or examination. Richard Slater was arrested on the day after the October election of last year, for what reason the Committee have been unable to ascertain, as he nor any one else ever knew. He was likewise imprisoned in the Government bastile at Indianapolis, and after four weeks close confinement was also discharged without a trial. Amos Green was arrested at Terre Haute on the 8th day of August, 1862, upon a telegraphic dispatch sent to Samuel Connor, the sheriff of Vigo county, by one John Logan, who was at that time, and still is, under various indictments for felony and misdemeanors. He was taken to Washington City, kept there for several days, and finally set at liberty, without accusation and without trial, and even then forced to pay his own expenses home. Mr. Slater and Mr. Reynolds are both ex-Senators, and Dr. Horton an ex-member of the House of Representatives of the State of Indiana. Perhaps no arrest has been more outrageous than that of Dr. Horton. He was spirited away at midnight, under the impression that he was going to perform an act of mercy; and thus kidnapped, he was hurried away from his home and family under circumstances that even precluded him from informing his anxious wife and children where he was until he had reached Indianapolis.

American citizens were thus harshly dealt with, simply because the weak and toppling party in power, in its madness to thrust its political heresies upon an intelligent and unwilling people, had established a system of espionage that gave any man, of the Administration school, the power to arrest and send to jail any one of his Democratic neighbors that, in his malice, prejudice, or misapprehension, he might wish to have put out of the way.

The public will not fail to notice the cases of Mr. Cassidy and Mr. Offutt, who were arrested in Rush county. Malignant despotism, of the most offensive and criminal nature, characterizes both these cases. The only pretended authority therefor was a *lettre-de-cachet* from Major-General Lewis Wallace, in command at Cincinnati—a letter in blank, assuming to confer upon an irresponsible itinerant telegraph operator the authority to go whithersoever he pleased, and arrest any citizen he might suspect of disloyalty. Respectful language can hardly portray this insolent impudence, this beggarly despotism, and this contemptable usurpation, so strangely and so outrageously mean, and so far below the standard of American citizenship. Against these prisoners no charge, not even a *false* affidavit, was preferred. It suited the caprice of a telegraph operator, acting in the capacity of a "*Deputy*

Major-General," to arrest them, and it was done. The dismal and dingy walls of the old French Bastile, which, for four hundred years, was used for the ruin of all who happened to incur the resentment and jealousy of tyrannical French monarchs, could not reveal more shocking instances of outrage and cruelty, than have been practiced throughout most of the northern States by various officers in the confidence of the present Administration.

Members of the Abolition party proper, who for twenty-three years have counseled a division of the Northern and Southern States—who have advised resistance to the laws of Congress and the interpretations of the Supreme Court—now hold most of the important and lucrative offices within the gift of Mr. Lincoln. And these are the men who are the most implacable and cruel toward all who do not sustain their folly and madness. Why did not the President arrest members of this party as well as members of the Democratic party? In the beginning of his term of office they said more, and did more, to embarrass his Administration than Democrats did. Wendall Phillips at Washington, the capital of the nation, within the hearing of the President and his cabinet, boldly said, "*I have labored for nineteen years to take nineteen States out of the Union.* * * * *I cursed the Constitution and the Union, and endeavored to break it, and thank God it is broken.*" The President could not have been ignorant that he had uttered these monstrous words. The Speaker of the House of Representatives occupied a place on the platform where the speech was delivered. Senators, in the confidence of the National Executive, were present. Republican members of Congress by scores, and citizens by hundreds, were there. The newspapers were full of it. Mr. Lincoln can not possibly escape upon the plea of ignorance. And this is not all. The next day after this reviler of the Constitution, this advocate of sedition, had uttered these wicked words, he made his appearance upon the floor of the United States Senate, in that sanctuary of constitutional liberty, consecrated for the greatest and wisest of all human purposes, still glorious with the recollections of the magical eloquence of Clay, the stately and overwhelming arguments of Webster, the parliamentary gladiature of Silas Wright, and Macy, and Hannegan, and Douglas—this leprous wretch presumed to go—and there, upon that sacred floor, the most illustrious theater the world has ever known—Wendall Phillips is greeted and formally welcomed by the Vice President of the United States, the second officer in position and honor in the whole republic. Let the intemperate partisans and the crazy fanatics, who are so especially puffed up with patriotism and consistency, take this notorious fact, in connection with a thousand other similar cases, and explain it to the satisfaction of the people, who, in the end, will be the arbiter of all these great questions. The whole matter is transparent. This Administration, itself inaugurated upon revolutionary principles, has, from the first hour of its installment, attempted to enforce submission to its usurpations. The people, long inured to free thought and free expression of thought, can not be put down now. It is madness to attempt it. They have been deceived by those having the control of public affairs, and they have denounced them for it, and their condemnations will continue as long as the offenses continue. The last Congress has been a disgrace to this nation. Its members—most of them—seem to have done every thing they could to irritate the people, and to destroy their liberties.

When the nation was bleeding at every pore—when one million of our brothers were engaged in mortal strife—when hoof of fire and sword of flame were scourging the land and making our rivers run red and thick with blood, these remorseless plunderers and robbers were engaged in schemes of self-aggrandizement, and in devising measures to increase our distractions in the States not in rebellion. Behold their record! The accumulated evidence that has been piled up mountain high against the thieving and jobbing villains that continually hang over the fallen, bleeding, struggling form of our liberties, like birds of evil prey, day and night, seeking some new quarry they may pounce upon and devour. They seem not to be satisfied with the gigantic rebellion that the armies and navy of the nation have been struggling for two years to subdue in the insurgent States, but they must exasperate the people here by the abolition of slavery in the District of Columbia —by the passage of a law permitting the testimony of negroes in certain cases against the whites—by the repeal of the law against the transportation of the mails by negroes—by the amendment of the law, so as to make it a high offense for an officer of the army to return a runaway slave to his master—by a refusal to make it an offense of like character for an officer to entice away a slave—by the passage of a law recognizing as our equals the negro governments of Liberia and Hayti—by the passage of a confiscation bill, aimed at slavery—by the passage of an act authorizing the President to call negroes into military service—by the passage of a law postponing the investigation of frauds against the Government for two years—by the passage of an unconstitutional indemnification act—in short, by a persistent and unremitting course of legislation that the country does not need, does not ask for, that is now denounced every day, and that sooner or later the people will overwhelm by repudiation and repeal. And the programme has been that all these wrongs must be endured by the people, or they should be arrested and imprisoned for it. "Eternal vigilence is the price of liberty." Let those in authority recollect that the American people learned that precept from one of clean hands and pure heart, at the feet of the greatest political Gamaliel of his age. They will not forget it as a principle, and they will not surrender it as a right.

We will next notice the arrests of citizens of Switzerland county. With all the care we have been able to bestow upon these cases, we have been unable to discover any cause for the arrest. The parties themselves know of none, and only conjecture that they were arrested because they were "Democrats, and did not agree with the President in regard to the manner of prosecuting the war." Several private citizens were seized, abused by vile epithets, and maltreated in various ways, imprisoned and half starved for many days, without any known cause. Among these prisoners was one who had been honored by his fellow citizens with distinction. Yet they were carried beyond the State, without legal authority, and at last discharged without a hearing.

Whatever may be said or thought, by the friends of the Governor of the State, in reference to arrests made upon the supposition that the draft law had been, or was about to be obstructed, there can, it appears to us, be but one opinion about his duty in regard to the arrests now under consideration. His duties are defined in the Constitution of the State. Among other things it is declared by that instrument that "*he shall take care that the laws be faithfully executed.*"—Art. 5, sec. 16, Const. of Ind. That he would faithfully discharge that duty was a part of his oath of office.—Art. 15, sect. 4, Const. of Ind. At that time we had on our statute book, (2 R. S., p. 400,) a section to the effect that it should be deemed a felony for any person "*forcibly and unlawfully to arrest any person and carry such person to parts without the State of Indiana,*" and the punishment was fine and the penitentiary. Plainly and without cavil this law was in those instances violated. There was not even the poor plea of the tyrant

—necessity, for the act. It was a palpable violation of the Constitution of the United States, fourth amendment, and that of Indiana, Art. 1, sec. 2, which were intended to secure the citizen against "unreasonable seizure."

In the face of all this, and of his sworn duty, the Governor did not move a finger to protect these citizens from arrest, or to obtain their release afterward. To the reverse the evidence tends to show that he was instrumental in procuring such arrests, *upon the representations of a man of such bad character, that he could not obtain a license to sell whisky.* We hope, for the dignity of the office Governor Morton accidentally fills, that there has been some misapprehension about this affair; but if the truth has been presented to us, into what a profound depth of infamy some men's partisan feelings will sink them.

Governor Morton has seen fit to pursue a very arbitrary and self-opinionated course in regard to the arrests made in Indiana. He has kept his lips sealed; but not one intelligent man, woman, or child in the State doubts that he has been the sole cause of every arrest that has been made—at all events, that he could have prevented every one of them, and had all violations of law, if any have been made, corrected by the Courts.

In an early period of the session of the Legislature, the following preamble and resolution was adopted:

"WHEREAS, The Secretary of War, in his last official report, has declared that the several arrests made throughout the various States were made by the advice and with the consent of the several Governors thereof; therefore, be it

"*Resolved*, That His Excellency, Governor O. P. Morton, be requested to furnish this House with the facts in regard to the arrests that have been made in the State of Indiana."

For sixty-one days the Legislature was in session, but not one word of reply did his Excellency, the Governor, ever make to the foregoing resolution. Who, then, has any doubt as to the cause of his silence?

We are unable to conjecture what kind of a defense the implicated parties will have to offer in answer to all this; but it will doubtless be the old plea of the tyrant—military necessity.

Republican journals, for the past year, have been crowded with allusions to the conduct of General Jackson at New Orleans. When or how these gentlemen have consented to make a model of this great hero of popular rights, the Committee have been unable to ascertain; doubtless, their enterprise commenced since the time they plastered every section corner-post of the land with the coffin handbills that were intended to cover his name and greatness with contumely and infamy.

But let us examine General Jackson's record a little, and see how far President Lincoln's case is similar to it. When General Jackson issued his proclamation in regard to the nullification of South Carolina, he also called the attention of Congress to the fact that South Carolina had sustained wrongs that must be cured. South Carolina complained of the tariff laws, and contended that they discriminated in favor of certain interests, prejudicial to her own, and upon this threatened nullification. General Jackson was equal to the emergency; but while he asserted the power of the Government to maintain its laws, he also recommended that the cause of complaint be eradicated. On the 4th day of December, 1832, he said: "What shall then be done? Large interests have grown up under the implied pledge of our national legislation, which it would seem a violation of public faith suddenly to abandon. *Nothing could justify it but the public safety, which is the supreme law.*"

General Jackson desired to sustain the Government, and he did sustain it, but he told Congress it must be done upon just and equitable principles.

How is President Lincoln's record on this score? For two years the Government has been engaged in prosecuting a great war—for what purpose? Because certain States have nullified the laws of the Government. How is it with a portion of the Northern States, who, in the beginning, were the most opposed to compromise, and the most in favor of war and the shedding of fraternal blood? How is it with Massachusetts? Has she never nullified the laws, and set at naught the Constitution? If her laws are to be legitimately understood, is she not this very day in a state of nullification? On her statute book, page 741, sec. 60, we find the following law:

"No person, while holding any office of honor, trust, or emolument, under the laws of this State, shall, in any capacity, take cognizance of any case, issue any warrant or other process, or grant any certificate, under or by virtue of an act of Congress, approved the 12th day of February, 1793, entitled 'An Act respecting fugitives from justice, and persons escaping from the service of their masters,' or under or by virtue of an act of Congress, approved the

18th day of September, 1850, entitled 'An Act to amend, and supplementary to 'An Act respecting fugitives from justice, and persons escaping from the service of their masters,' or shall in any capacity serve such warrant or other process. Any justice of the peace, who offends against the provisions of this section, by directly or indirectly acting in such cases, shall forfeit a sum not exceeding one thousand dollars, or be imprisoned in jail not exceeding one year for each offense.'"

There is the law as it stands on the statute book this day. Has Mr. Lincoln, like Jackson, ever advised its repeal, that the Northern States in prosecuting a gigantic war against the Southern States, might do it with clean hands! He has done nothing of the kind. On the contrary, this little, seditious, plodding, plundering State of Massachusetts has controlled the whole policy of this war. And in doing this, she has made the war a means of speculation. Her delegates in Congress have devised more draft laws and conscription laws than all the other States put together—and yet how does she stand on the record? The population of the State of Indiana, as evidenced by the late census reports, is 1,300,000, and the population of Massachusetts 1,200,000 in round numbers, and yet Indiana, under the various calls of the President, and by draft, has furnished the United States army 102,000 soldiers, and Massachusetts only about 70,000—the draft law, too, be it remembered, was strictly enforced in Indiana, and is not, to this day, completed in Massachusetts.

But the President is justified by his adherents, under the omnipotent plea of "military necessity." They do not pretend to put any limitations upon it, and all who do not agree that the proposition is correct, are summarily denounced as disloyal. If these gentlemen would consent to read and reflect a little, they would discover they are at war with the principles of the greatest, the wisest, and the most learned law writers who have treated of this subject.

In Johnson *v.* Duncan, 3 Martin, 531, Judge Derbigny says: "To have a correct idea of martial law in a free country, examples must not be sought in the arbitrary conduct of absolute governments. The monarch who unites in his person *all* the powers, may delegate to his generals an authority as unbounded as his own. But in a Republic, where the constitution has fixed the extent and limits of every branch of the government in time of war, as well as of peace, there can exist nothing vague, uncertain, or arbitrary, in the exercise of any authority. Can it be asserted, that while British subjects are secured against oppression in the worst times, American citizens are left at the mercy of the will of an individual who may, in certain cases, *the necessity of which is to be judged of by himself*, assume a supreme, overbearing, unbounded power! The idea is not only repugnant to the principles of any free government, but subversive of the very foundations of our own."

Sir Edward Coke says: "If a lieutenant, or other that hath commission of martial authority, in time of peace, hang, or otherwise execute, any man by color of martial law, *this is murder;* for this is against Magna Charta, chap. 29, and is done with such power and strength as the party can not defend himself; and here the law implieth malice." 3 Inst. 52, 53.

Sir William Blackstone says: "For martial law, which is built upon no settled principles, but is entirely arbitrary in its decisions, is, as Sir Matthew Hale observes, in truth and reality, no law; but is something indulged in rather than allowed as a law. The necessity of order and discipline, *in an army*, is the only thing which can give it countenance."

Lord Mansfield says: "To lay down, in an English court of justice, such a monstrous proposition as that a Governor, acting by virtue of letters patent under the Great Seal, is accountable only to God and his own conscience; that he is absolutely despotic, and can spoil, plunder, and affect his majesty's subjects, both in their liberty and property, with impunity, is a doctrine that can not be maintained."—Cowp. 175.

Chief Justice Taney says: "The movement upon Chihuahau was undoubtedly undertaken from high and patriotic motives. It was boldly planned and gallantly executed, and contributed to the successful issue of the war. But it is not for the court to say what protection or indemnity is due from the public to an officer who, in his zeal for the honor and interest of his country, and in the excitement of military operations, has trespassed upon private rights. That question belongs to the political department of the Government. *Our duty is to determine under what circumstances private property may be taken from the owner, by a military officer, in time of war. And the question here is, whether the law permits it to be taken to insure the success of any enterprise against a public enemy which the commanding officer may deem it advisable to undertake. And we think it very clear that the law does not permit it.*"—13 How. 135.

Read what General Washington says: "That every officer and soldier will constantly bear in mind that he comes to support the laws, and that it would be peculiarly unbecoming in him to be, in any way, the infractor of them; *that the essential principles of free government confine the province of the military, when called forth on such occasions, to two objects;* first, to combat and subdue all who may be found *in arms* in opposition to the national will and authority; secondly, to aid and support the *civil magistrates* in bringing offenders to justice. THE DISPENSATION OF THIS JUSTICE BELONGS TO THE CIVIL MAGISTRATES; AND LET IT EVER BE OUR PRIDE AND OUR GLORY TO LEAVE THE SACRED DEPOSITE THERE INVIOLATE."—Irving's Life of Washington, vol. 5, chap. 25.

General Washington never sanctioned the doctrine that martial law could be declared over American citizens. In his Farewell Address he took precisely the opposite ground of this theory. Here is what he said on that question: "It is important, likewise, that the habits of thinking, in a free country, should inspire caution in those intrusted with its administration, to confine themselves within their respective constitutional spheres; avoiding, in the exercise of the powers of one department, to encroach upon another. *The spirit of encroachment tends to consolidate the powers of all the departments in one, and thus to create, whatever the form of government, a real despotism.* A just estimate of that love of power and proneness to abuse it which predominates in the human heart, is sufficient to satisfy us of the truth of this position. The necessity of reciprocal checks in the exercise of political power, by dividing and distributing it into different depositories, and constituting each the guardian of the public weal against the invasions of the other, has been evinced by experiments, ancient and modern, some of them in our own country, and under our own eyes. *To preserve them must be as necessary as to institute them.* If, in the opinion of the people, the distribution or modification of the constitutional powers be in any particular wrong, let it be corrected by an amendment in the way in which the Constitution designates. BUT LET THERE BE NO CHANGE BY USURPATION; FOR THOUGH THIS, IN ONE INSTANCE, MAY BE THE INSTRUMENT OF GOOD, IT IS THE CUSTOMARY WEAPON BY WHICH FREE GOVERNMENTS ARE DESTROYED. THE PRECEDENTS MUST, ALWAYS, GREATLY OVERBALANCE, IN PERMAMENT EVIL, ANY PARTIAL OR TRANSIENT BENEFIT WHICH THE USE CAN, AT ANY TIME, YIELD."

In regard to General Jackson's connection with the New Orleans affair, in which the friends of this Administration find so much to justify President Lincoln for the absurd and despotic course he has seen fit to pursue, the Committee would refer the reader to a very able paper prepared on this subject by one of the ripest lawyers and most proficient statesmen of Ohio. We give the following extract:

"There is no question that on the 16th of December, 1814, General Jackson declared the city of New Orleans and its environs to be under 'strict' martial law; but, inasmuch as he was then acting as a military commander, in charge of the seventh military district, the precedent (granting all that has been claimed for it) can be of no avail unless sanctioned by the Government of the United States as a lawful exercise of power. The truth is, however, that the Government did not sanction it, and expressly disapproved it. (Letter of the Secretary of War to General Jackson, April 12, 1815.) The reason why no further notice was taken of the affair at the time is, that Jackson submitted, like a patriot and real soldier as he was, the moment his error was pointed out.

"He never claimed authority to suspend the privilege of *habeas corpus*, except in the city of New Orleans and its immediate neighborhood, and while invasion was actual or imminent. He never dreamed, for an instant, of such enormous and inexcusable usurpations as we now see, almost every where, and on all occasions, practiced by military commanders. The acts of Congress then in force gave him a right to call upon the State of Louisiana for the services of every able-bodied citizen; and he had, with the assent of the State authorities, placed all who were capable of bearing arms under orders to be in readiness, as soldiers, upon brief and sudden notice. It was upon the idea that he thus commanded the entire population, as persons liable to military duty at once, and therefore subject to military law, and not upon the notion (at present so much in vogue) that a General can, by proclamation or otherwise, constitute himself an irresponsible dictator over the lives and liberties of his fellow-citizens, that Jackson assumed to act."

General Jackson himself, in his address of March 3, 1837, has given to the American people some serious admonitions upon the subject now under discussion. He says:—"It is well known that there have always been among us those who wish to enlarge the powers of the General Government; and experience would seem to indicate that there is a tendency on the part of this Government to overstep the boundaries marked out for it by the Constitution. Its legitimate authority is abundantly sufficient for all the purposes for which it was created; and its powers being expressly enumerated, there can be no justification for claiming any thing beyond them. *Every attempt to exercise power beyond these limits should be promptly and firmly opposed. For one evil example will lead to other measures still more mischievous; and if the principle of constructive powers, or supposed advantages, or temporary circumstances, shall ever be permitted to justify the assumption of a power not given by the Constitution, the General Government will, before long, absorb all the powers of legislation, and you will have, in effect, but one consolidated Government.* From the extent of our country, its diversified interests, different pursuits and different habits, it is too obvious for argument that a single consolidated government would be wholly inadequate to watch over and protect its interests; *and every friend of our free institutions should be always prepared to maintain unimpaired and in full vigor, the rights and sovereignty of the States, and to confine the action of the General Government strictly to the sphere of its appropriate duties.*"

Thomas Jefferson has also left on record certain admonitions with reference to this subject that the true friends of Democratical principles will never cease to respect. In a letter he wrote at Paris to Mr. Donald, February 7, 1788, he expresses the wish that certain States would insist upon a declaration of rights in the final ratifiication of the Constitution of the United States.

"By a declaration of rights," said this great philosopher, "I mean one which shall stipulate freedom of religion, freedom of the press, freedom of commerce against monopolies, trial by juries in all cases, *no suspension of the habeas corpus*, no standing armies. THESE ARE FETTERS AGAINST DOING EVIL WHICH NO HONEST GOVERNMENT SHOULD DECLINE."

On the 4th day of March, 1801, Mr. Jefferson insisted upon the following fundamental principles of government under our Constitution, and, as he was one of its original framers, he certainly better knew what it means than Mr. Lincoln does.

"*The Supremacy of the Civil over the Military Authority.*"

"*The Arraignment of all abuses at the bar of Public Reason.*"

"*Freedom of the Press.*"

"FREEDOM OF PERSON, UNDER THE PROTECTION OF THE HABEAS CORPUS."

Trial by Juries Impartially Selected."

"These principles" said the great Jefferson, "form the bright constellation which has gone before us, and guided our steps through the age of revolution and reformation. The wisdom of our sages, and the blood of our heroes have been devoted to their attainment. They should be the creed of our political faith, the text of civil instruction, *the touchstone by which to try the services of those we trust.* AND SHOULD WE WANDER FROM THEM, IN MOMENTS OF ERROR AND ALARM, LET US HASTEN TO RETRACE OUR STEPS, AND TO REGAIN THE ROAD WHICH ALONE LEADS TO PEACE, LIBERTY, AND SAFETY."

But the Committee decline to pursue this discussion any further, the evidence is given in full—the public may take it and weigh it for themselves. Afterwhile they will pass their verdict upon it—when those now in power will be brought back to a just realization THAT THE PEOPLE ARE THE GOVERNMENT, AND THAT THEY WILL NEVER YIELD UP THEIR PRECIOUS LIBERTIES—NEVER.

JASON B. BROWN,
BAYLESS W. HANNA,
O. S. GIVEN,
JONAS G. HOWARD,
EDWIN P. FERRIS,
CHARLES B. LASSELLE,
SAMUEL A. SHOAFF.

EVIDENCE.

CASE OF DR. THEODORE HORTON.

Dr. Theodore Horton being first duly sworn, testified as follows:

Question by Mr. Howard—

State when, where, and in what manner you were arrested, together with your name, age, occupation, your place of residence, and for what period you have lived at your present place of residence, and where and how long you were held in custody.

Answer—My name is Theodore Horton. I am thirty-nine years of age; a practicing physician; reside at Bluffton, Wells county, State of Indiana; have resided there for the last fifteen years. I was arrested by W. H. Fitch on or about the 9th day of October, 1862, upon an order from D. G. Rose. On that night, at about eleven o'clock, and some time after I had retired to bed, I was aroused by a loud knock at my door; I bade the person to step in, and upon his doing so, I inquired what he wanted; he informed me that he wanted the assistance of a surgeon, as a friend had broke his leg, about three miles from town, on the road to Murray. I inquired the name of the person who had broke his leg, and was informed that it was Johnson. I then said that I knew of no person of that name living in that vicinity, when I was informed that he was a stranger, and that he was on his way to Bluffton riding in a covered carriage, and in the darkness of the night they had unfortunately upset, thrown him out and broken his leg. The messenger, who proved to be W. H. Fitch, informed me that he had his carriage at my door, and if I saw proper I could ride with him. I tried to excuse myself, but Fitch insisted, and I finally consented to ride with him on condition that he would bring me back after I had performed his service. This he gave me the fullest assurance he would do. I then got into his carriage, and took the back seat. Mr. Fitch got in beside, and a person whom I afterward learned was Frank Burrass, got in, and seating himself upon the front seat, took up the reins and drove off. We had gone about two miles from town, when Mr. Fitch remarked, as he was sitting upon my left side, that his arm was very sore beating against the side of the carriage; that he would be glad to exchange seats with me. I at once complied with his request, and changed seats with him. As soon as he had become seated, he said: "It is no use keeping this thing from you any longer. I am an officer, and have been sent by Provost Marshal Rose to arrest you, and bring you at once before him at his office in Indianapolis." I told him that I regretted that he had made the arrest in the manner he had, but would be better satisfied if he would turn back and let me inform my family where I was going, that they might not feel so uneasy about my absence, and also that I might have an opportunity to make some necessary changes in my apparel. Mr. Fitch informed me that it was out of the question, as he had to be at Huntington at 5 o'clock, A. M., to meet the train, and that he would not miss it for a hundred dollars. I then inquired for his authority. He informed me that he had it, but the darkness of the night being made impenetrable by clouds and rain, I could not read it until we arrived at some place where we could have the convenience of a light, which did not occur until we reached Huntington. Here Mr. Fitch put into my hands an order, issued by Marshal Rose, directing Messrs. Fitch and Bisbing to arrest me and bring me before him, at his office at Indianapolis. No crime was alleged or charge made, and Mr. Fitch informed me that he was entirely ignorant as to what the offense was upon which the arrest was made. At Huntington we got in company with Bisbing, who had accompanied Mr. Fitch to assist in making the arrest, but, in consequence of indisposition, was compelled to remain at that place.

In about three hours the train for Peru arrived, and I was put on board, and brought to Indianapolis. I was taken to the Federal Building and delivered to Marshal Rose, who conducted me to an apartment in the building and locked me in by myself. I remained here about three days, before I was aware of what the nature of the charge was for which I had been arrested and thrown into prison. Then, at my request, Marshal Rose brought forward an affidavit made by one John Phipps, an entirely irresponsible person, alleging that upon a certain occasion I had made use of language calculated to discourage enlistments.

I at once desired an examination, knowing the charge to be

most flagitiously false, and believing that they were founded in personal malice, made alone for the purpose of gratifying the basest passions of human nature, and perfecting a political conspiracy and intrigue, through the flagrant usurpation of power by government officials. But all efforts to obtain an investigation were unsuccessful, and after being kept in confinement for five weeks, was released by Marshal Rose, who informed me I was "a free man," and was "at liberty to go where I pleased." It is my impression that the affidavit of Phipps was made on the sixth day of October last, and I was arrested on the ninth of the same month.

Question by Mr. Hanna—

State whether you ever made a request for examination or trial as to the causes of your imprisonment?

Answer—Yes, sir; I requested Mr. Rose to inform me; and I thought Mr. Rose had a discretionary power in the matter. My attorneys told me they could do nothing, as there were no precedents in law—no law governing the case.

Question by Mr. Hanna—

State what Mr. Rose's response was to your question in that matter?

Answer—He said he had no discretionary power, but that he had telegraphed to Washington City, to the authorities there, for instruction, and was awaiting a response, expecting it from day to day, until the period of my release, for some weeks. For the first week or two, we were questioning him from day to day.

Question by Mr. Hanna—

State whether at any time during your duress, Mr. Rose ever informed you by what authority you had been arrested, and by what authority he acted in the premises?

Answer—He never did.

Question by Mr. Hanna—

State whether you ever had any conversation with Governor Morton on the subject of your arrest during your confinement?

Answer—Not during my confinement.

Question by Mr. Hanna—

Is the affidavit upon which you were arrested in your possession?

Answer—It is not.

Question by Mr. Hanna—

Do you remember the substance of that affidavit?

Answer—I do not recollect its date, but I do recollect the substance of it.

Question by Mr. Hanna—

State the contents of the affidavit as near as you can recollect?

Answer—It asserted that in the speech that I made that this was an Abolition war, and that Abe Lincoln's proclamation of September 22, capped the climax of the Abolition policy; that in appealing to the audience I asked them whether they would enlist to fight to free the negroes, and that I responded myself to the question, "no, no! you will not." This was about the substance of it, but there were other points I do not remember.

Question by Mr. Hanna—

Do you know Phipps, the affiant you have alluded to, when you see him?

Answer—Yes sir, I do.

Question by Mr. Hanna—

Was he present at the time you made this speech referred to?

Answer—He was.

Question by Mr. Hanna—

Are you acquainted with his general character in the neighborhood where he lives for truth and veracity?

Answer—I am.

Question by Mr. Hanna—

What is it?

Answer—It is bad.

Question by Mr. Hanna—

Are you acquainted with his condition as to means and property?

Answer—I am.

Question by Mr. Hanna—

State whether he is responsible for his contracts?

Answer—He is irresponsible.

Question by Mr. Hanna—

Do I understand you to say you were arrested on the night of the ninth of October?

Answer—Yes, sir; I was.

Question by Mr. Hanna—

About what time?

Answer—About eleven o'clock, p. m.

Question by Mr. Hanna—

When were you discharged?

Answer—I think it was about the thirteenth day of November.

Question by Mr. Hanna—

Did they pay your expenses home after your discharge?

Answer—I paid my own expenses.

Question by Mr. Hanna—

State what conversation occurred between you and Colonel Rose, or any other officer having you in duress, at the time of your discharge?

Answer—All the conversation that took place between myself and Colonel Rose, at the time of my discharge, was this: he said "I have the pleasure to inform you that you are a free man. You are at liberty to go where you please."

Question by Mr. Hanna—

State when and where you made the speech alluded to in Phipp's affidavit.

Answer—In Nottingham township, Wells county, Indiana. The precise day I do not remember. It was about the second day of October last.

Question by Mr. Hanna—

Did you, at any time after your arrest upon Phipps' affidavit, have any trial or examination before any court or officer whatsoever, as to the causes of your arrest?

Answer—No, sir; I was discharged without any trial.

Question by Mr. Brown—

What was the occupation of Colonel Rose at the time of your arrest and imprisonment?

Answer—He was acting as Provost, and U. S. Marshal, for the District of Indiana.

Question by Mr. Given—

State what is the age of Mr. Phipps; if he is an able-bodied man, and what political party he acts with, and belongs to?

Answer—I should judge him to be a man of about thirty years of age, able-bodied, and a Republican.

Question by Mr. Given—

State what political party you acted with at the time of your arrest?

Answer—With the Democratic party. I never acted with any other.

Question by Mr. Hanna—

State, Doctor, whether you ever made the declarations alleged against you in Phipps' affidavit?

Answer—I did not, as quoted in the affidavit.

Question by Mr. Hanna—

State whether it was your purpose, in the speech referred to, to embarrass enlistments under the order of the President of the United States?

Answer—I had no thought, intention, or desire of doing so.

Question by Mr. Brown—

State whether you did not produce to Colonel Rose the affidavit of several of your responsible neighbors, who heard the speech referred to in Phipps' affidavit, alleging that the statements in Phipps' affidavit were false?

Answer—I produced to Colonel Rose an affidavit, with the signatures of sixteen persons who heard the speech referred to by Phipps, and one or two other affidavits, asserting that the statements made by Phipps, in his said affidavit, were false, and the persons who made these affidavits were all citizens of the immediate neighborhood in which the speech was made.

Question by Mr. Gregory—

State by whom this meeting was called, and what was the object of the same, at which you made the speech alluded to.

Answer—The meeting was called by the candidate upon the Republican ticket for Representative, A. B. Jetmore, and was called for the purpose of discussing the political topics of the day.

Question by Mr. Gregory—

By whom were you called out to make a speech upon that occasion?

Answer—By the Democrats living in the vicinity of the place where the speech was made.

Question by Mr. Gregory—

State, as near as you can, what was your language in regard to the policy of the present Administration, in carrying on this war, as to the negro question?

Answer—As near as I can recollect, I stated that I believed that it was the policy of this Administration to abolish slavery, and that I considered that Abolitionism was as much opposed to the existence of the Union as Secessionism; that I considered in the conflict which then overwhelmed the country, that we had enemies at the North as well as at the South; that we proposed to meet these enemies in the North at the ballot-box, and by the little paper ballots, which drop as the silent snow-flake, to sweep the Abolition minions from power; and while we thus relieved the Government from their oppressive hands, it was also our duty to shoulder our muskets and put down Secessionism with bullets.

Question by Mr. GREGORY—

State when you were first shown the affidavit upon which you were arrested?

Answer—I think it was on the 14th or 15th of October, a few days after I was arrested.

Question by Mr. GREGORY—

State how you were treated, as to privileges granted you, while you were in the custody of the United States Marshal.

Answer—I could not complain of the treatment.

Question by Mr. BAKER—

How long before you were released from confinement that you received the affidavits stating that Phipps' affidavit was false?

Answer—About three weeks.

Question by Mr. BAKER—

Have you the affidavits?

Answer—I have them at home.

Question by Mr. BAKER—

Did these men who made the affidavits contradicting Phipps' affidavit, know the language that Phipps had employed in the affidavit he made against you upon which you were arrested?

Answer—I procured a copy of Phipps' affidavit and sent it to them, and suppose they did.

Question by Mr. GREGG—

Did Colonel Rose know any thing about what the affidavit you handed him contained?

Answer—Only what I told him, and that was that they were the affidavits of citizens who were at the meeting spoken of by Phipps, contradicting Phipps' statements. When I handed the affidavits to Rose, he said that he had not time to examine them. He took them and laid them on the mantle-piece, and I then told him that if he could not examine them that I would keep them in my possession until he had time to examine them. He never called for them.

Question by Mr. HANNA—

State whether or not you have, at any time during the present hostilities, endeavored, by your personal influence and your means, to assist the Government in procuring recruits for the army of the United States?

Answer—I have, by assisting companies with money as they

were about to leave our place, and so assisted in getting up recruits at meetings called for that purpose.

Question by Mr. SHOAFF—

Was there more than one affidavit made against you embodying the substance of Phipps' affidavit?

Answer—I don't know that there were others.

Question by Mr. SHOAFF—

Did you understand at the time that there was an order of the Secretary of War making the discouragement of enlistments a penal offense?

Answer—I did.

Question by Mr. BROWN—

State whether during your imprisonment there were any other persons imprisoned with you upon charges similar to the one upon which you were imprisoned; and if so, who were they?

Answer—There were two others confined in the same room with me upon similar charges—Richard Slater, of Dearborn county, and Harris Reynolds, of Fountain county.

Question by Mr. BROWN—

Were they discharged at the same time, and in the same manner, that you were?

Answer—Mr. Slater was, but Mr. Reynolds was discharged some two weeks prior to our discharge, and I understand upon condition that he would furnish a substitute for himself in the army, he being drafted.

Question by Mr. BROWN—

Are you certain that you were arrested and imprisoned before the State election?

Answer—I am; some three days before the election.

Question by Mr. BAKER—

What company was it you assisted, by money or otherwise, in getting off to the army?

Answer—I assisted Captain Peter Studebaker's company, and some five others, which were raised in our county.

Question by Mr. BAKER—

In what manner did you assist them?

Answer—In giving money to assist the companies off; and being the leader of a band of music, furnished free music at numerous meetings called for the purpose of soliciting volunteers; and in escorting companies on their road to Indianapolis.

Question by Mr. LASSELLE—

State if you, during your imprisonment, were called as a physician to visit some of the Blackford county prisoners, who were sick in other rooms; and if so, your judgment as to their treatment, the cause of their illness, &c.

Answer—I was so called by Colonel Rose; I found them confined in very small cells, in which there were no side windows; but a small, closed sky-light; no ventilation except through the small interstices of the iron doors. The rooms were filthy, and not fit for the confinement of prisoners. I found several of them seriously ill, and attribute their disease to the unhealthiness of the prison—perhaps aggravated by improper diet.

THEODORE HORTON.

STATE OF INDIANA, } ss:
Wells County, }

We, Jerome Ruff, John M. Powers, Rannals Walser, George J. Gottschalk, John Gottschalk, George Dulinsky, Wm. Dulinsky, Matthew Long, Cyrus Marsh, Benneville Sawyer, John A. Sawyer, Amos Gehrett, and E. A. Horton, of lawful age, residents of the county and State aforesaid, upon our oaths depose and say: That on the 2d day of October, 1862, we attended a political meeting in Nottingham township, Wells county, Indiana, which said meeting was appointed for the purpose of discussing the political issues before the country, by one A. B. Jetmore, candidate for State Representative for the counties of Blackford and Wells; that one John Phipps, of company A, Thirty-Fourth Regiment Indiana Volunteer Infantry, was present at said meeting, for the purpose of procuring volunteers; that Theodore Horton, (now under arrest upon a charge of then and there discouraging enlistments, which said charge said Phipps, on the 6th of October, 1862, made affidavit to before one Dwight Klinck, a notary public in and for said county and State,) was also present at said meeting; that said Horton, after said Jetmore and said Phipps had concluded their efforts on the occasion, was called for by a large number present, to address them; that said Horton distinctly inquired, before he responded to that call, if said Jetmore and said Phipps had concluded their labors for the evening, and not until he had received from those gentlemen an affirmative response to his said inquiry, did said Horton proceed to address said meeting. And deponents say that their understanding of the purpose of said Horton being so called upon to address said meeting, and of his responding to said call, was to answer said Jetmore's political speech, and for such purpose only.

Deponents further say, they were present during the entire remarks of said Horton then and there made; that they paid strict and close attention to those remarks; that if the language imputed to said Horton by said Phipps in his said affidavit, to-wit: "I always knew this was an Abolition war—the President's proclamation tops the Abolition climax—you have been asked to-night to volunteer—did you do it? No, you are not a-going to volunteer. The speaker called for volunteers—how many did he get? None. You are not going to volunteer under such a policy—no, not one. The persons in power are all Abolitionists, and all who uphold the Administration in its policy are Abolitionists. We will put the Democrats in power, and then we will shoot down the Abolitionists," had been used by said Horton then and there, deponents would remember it; that said Horton did not use said language, nor any language calculated to discourage enlistments, but on the contrary, said Horton then and there spoke in substance as follow, to wit: "That the country had been forced into this war by the disunion Abolitionists of the North and the fire-eating Secessionists of the South; that there was left us but one course, namely, to shoulder our muskets and destroy the rebels of the South with bullets, and to meet the Abolitionists at the ballot-box, and by the mighty power of those little paper ballots, which drop as the silent snow-flake, to sweep from power the Abolition element in the Government, and restore it to the glory and power in which our fathers bequeathed it to us;" that said Horton then and there uttered no language expressing hostility to the Government, or calculated to discourage enlistments, unless the foregoing be so regarded.

And deponents further say that, in answer to an inquiry then and there put to him by said Jetmore, in substance, whether or not he, said Horton, was in favor of putting down the Rebellion, said Horton distinctly and emphatically said "he *was* in favor of putting down the Rebellion, and that the war should be carried on until that purpose was accomplished."

Deponents further say that there were present at said meeting about thirty or forty persons.

And further deponents say not.

JEROME B. RUFF,
JOHN M. POWERS,
RANNALS WALSER,
GEORGE J. GOTTSCHALK,
JOHN GOTTSCHALK, 18 years old,
GEORGE DULINSKY, 17 years old,
WILLIAM DULINSKY,
MATHEW LONG,

CYRUS MARSH,
BENNEVILLE SAWYER,
JOHN A. SAWYER,
AMOS GEHRETT,
E. A. HORTON.

State of Indiana, Wells Connty, ss :

Personally appeared before me, the undersigned Justice of the Peace, in and for said county, Jerome B. Ruff, John M. Powers, Rannals Walser, George J. Gottschalk, John Gottschalk, George Dulinsky, William Dulinsky, Mathew Long, Cyrus Marsh, Benneville Sawyer, and John A. Sawyer, and subscribed and made oath to the foregoing affidavit, this 17th of October, 1862.

In testimony whereof, I hereunto set my hand and seal, this 17th day of October, 1862.

DAVID MYERS, J. P.

THE BLACKFORD COUNTY CASES.

ANDREW BRICKLEY AFFIRMED.

Examined by Mr. Ferris—

Answer—My name is Andrew Brickley; age thirty-three years. I reside at Hartford City, Blackford county, Indiana. I have resided in Blackford county about eight years, and in the town of Hartford City about two years. My occupation is that of a saddler and harness maker; I am, at present, sheriff of Blackford county.

I was arrested by Thomas Browne, of Winchester, at Hartford City, on or about the 8th of October, 1862, upon a charge, as Browne alleged, that I had aided and abetted in resisting the draft. In making the arrest, he said that he arrested me upon affidavits that had been filed by citizens against me, but refused to show me any authority for making the arrest. Browne was accompanied by a file of soldiers some ten or twelve strong, under his command. After my arrest I was taken to Indianapolis, by soldiers detailed for that purpose. Then I was placed in the Government Bastile—that is the Post Office Building—placed in the fourth story of that building—there locked up, without fire, bedding, or any convenience of the kind. Soldiers without the doors guarded the entrance. There were six of us confined in that cell. We had no fire during our stay in the building—some thirty-three days. We had bedding, however, after the third night. We were released on or about the 15th of November last. At the time of our release, an Irishman named John ———, a waiter or servant of Colonel Rose, who sometimes carried the keys, came in and said to us that we were now released, but wished us to tarry, as Marshal Rose might wish to have some conversation with us before we left. We told him that we would cheerfully do so, and requested that he might call, so that we could have a conversation with him. We waited some two hours, but he did not come. Then John stated to us that we could leave, as the Marshal was not coming. We then left the prison-rooms and returned home. We paid all our expenses home. The food furnished us, while in prison, consisted generally of old bacon, sometimes very badly tainted, and sea biscuit or pilot bread, and occasionally baker's bread. We had nothing to eat with—as knives, forks, and spoons—until some of our friends brought them. We also ourselves, in consequence of the bad food furnished us, had to purchase our own provisions out.

In consequence of this imprisonment my health was seriously impaired for several months. From cold and exposure I contracted cold, which settled upon my lungs, and until within the last three weeks, I have been unable to do a day's work.

Question by Mr. LASSELLE—

Who is the Mr. Browne you allude to as having arrested you?

Answer—Thomas Browne, of Winchester, who is now a Senator here from Randolph county.

Question by Mr. GIVEN—

Were you acquainted with Browne prior to your arrest?

Answer—Not very intimately. I knew him by sight.

Question by Mr. LASSELLE—

State whether at the time of your arrest you demanded of Browne his authority for arresting you.

Answer—I did. His reply was, I have not arrested you without affidavit; I have the affidavit of several of the citizens of this place; but refused to show his authority.

Question by Mr. GIVEN—

Do you know who the persons were that made the affidavit?

Answer—I do not know only from rumor.

Question by Mr. FERRIS—

State the facts in regard to the truth or falsity of the charge that you aided and abetted in resisting the draft.

Answer—It is utterly false that I did either; on the contrary, on the day the ballot-box was mashed, I used all my energies to prevent the trouble, and twice succeeded in getting the prime mover in the difficulty out of the court-house, and was myself at the time of the mashing outside of the court-house.

Question by Mr. FERRIS—

What did you do toward getting a hearing, and with what success?

Answer—We urged a hearing, but got none.

Question by Mr. FERRIS—

What was your treatment after your arrest and until your incarceration in prison here?

Answer—On our way here we were guarded by soldiers and refused the privilege of conversing with each other. Upon our arrival in this city we were marched through the streets, and held at the street corners for some time as if on exhibition, and then we were marched through the camp.

Question by Mr. Lasselle—

State by what authority or by what officer you were detained in prison, so far as you know or believe.

Answer—My opinion is that it was by authority of Marshal Rose, and my reason for this opinion is that those who had the custody of us quoted him as authority.

Question by Mr. Given—

Have you a family?

Answer—Yes, sir; a wife and three children.

Question by Mr. Given—

What political party did you at that time belong to?

Answer—The Democratic party.

Question by Mr. Given—

State, if you know, to what party Mr. Browne, who arrested you, belongs.

Answer—I understand he belongs to the Republican party.

Question by Mr. Gregory—

At or before the draft in your county, do you know any thing about any secret organizations in your county to resist the draft?

Answer—I do not.

Question by Mr. Gregory—

Did any one in your county before the draft, secretly or otherwise, advise or counsel with you what to do in permitting the draft to be carried out in your county?

Answer—They did not.

Question by Mr. Gregory—

State whether you were called upon by the Provost Marshal to assist him in completing the draft, and did you so assist him?

Answer—I was called upon merely to stand by and see that it was done legally and right—not asked to participate in the drawing. The request was from the Provost Marshal. I stood by the Commissioner when the drafting commenced, but left the room, taking with me the leading man in the disturbance, Williams, out of the house, and having taken him out the second time, he slipped me, and the draft-box was mashed up while I was out of doors.

Question by Mr. GREGORY—

Did you refuse to act as the Deputy of the Provost Marshal in making the draft in that county?

Answer—Yes sir; I did refuse to take any part in the drawing, further than to stand by and see that it was legally done, as I have before stated.

Question by Mr. GREGORY—

State whether this Williams, who resisted the draft, was arrested for his conduct?

Answer—Not to my knowledge.

Question by Mr. GREGORY—

Did you, as Sheriff, do any thing to cause said Williams to be arrested?

Answer—I did not.

Question by Mr. GREGORY—

State why?

Answer—I had no warrant to do so, and beside this, I was arrested the second day after myself.

Question by Mr. GREGORY—

State whether you caused or directed any one on the day of the difficulty to pursue and capture said Williams?

Answer—I did not.

Question by Mr. FERRIS—

Was the Provost Marshal himself present at the time of the draft, and if so, did he order the arrest of said Williams?

Answer—He was present, but did not, to my knowledge, give such an order.

Question by Mr. FERRIS—

Why did you not arrest Williams?

Answer—I considered I had no legal right to do so. I was not acting as Provost Marshal, nor as his Deputy; did not see the draft-box broken, and had no lawful warrant to make an arrest.

Question by Mr. FERRIS—

You have, in your testimony, alluded to your action in endeavoring to quiet Williams, who mashed the box. Now state what occasioned Williams' dissatisfaction? What did he say was the trouble?

Answer—He complained that he had been enrolled in the wrong township—a township he did not reside in. The township in which he alleged he should have been enrolled, was subject to a draft of only *two* men, while that in which he actually was enrolled required a draft of *thirty-eight* men. Williams' statement as to his residence was correct, and the necessary change of his location was made prior to the attempt to execute the draft.

ANDREW BRICKLEY.

FRANK M. TAUGHINBAUGH SWORN.

Examined by Mr. Lasselle—

Answer—F. M. Taughinbaugh. I am in my thirty-third year; a farmer; my residence is in Blackford county. I have resided there, mainly, for eighteen years. I have a family—a wife and three children.

I was arrested at midnight on the 9th of October last, at my own house, some ten miles and a half from Hartford City, by a file of eight soldiers, under the orders, as I understood, of Thomas Browne, of Winchester, in Randolph county. Upon my arrest, I demanded their authority and the cause for my arrest. This was refused. On the next morning they started with me for Indianapolis, where we arrived on the 11th of that month. At Indianapolis we were placed in the cells of the Post Office prison. I have heard read the statements of Mr. Brickley, before this Committee, and I corroborate his testimony as to our incarceration in prison, treatment, and final release, having been confined with him in the same room, and released in the same manner, and at the same time, and by the same person. The charge, as I learned after my arrival in this city, was, that I had participated, or aided and abetted, in resisting the draft at Hartford City. The charge was wholly false. I did nothing of the kind.

I knew of no secret organizations at the time, designed or intended to resist the draft, nor do I believe there was any. I saw the draft-box mashed, and saw but one man (Williams,) engaged in it. I saw the sheriff (Brickley) take Williams out of the room twice, and know that he used his efforts to prevent the mashing of the draft-box.

Question by Mr. Ferris—

State what, if any, efforts you made to procure a hearing in your case, or a release.

Answer—I asked the guards who had charge of us, when our trial was going off; and they said they knew nothing more about it than we did.

Question by Mr. SHOAFF—

Did you, at any time, send a written communication to the Marshal, demanding a hearing?

Answer—I did not.

Question by Mr. FERRIS—

Did you ever apply to any person having you in charge for the affidavits filed against you, and, if so, with what success?

Answer—We employed Judge Roache to do so; and he informed us that he could not get to see them.

Question by Mr. FERRIS—

What was your treatment, by those who had you in custody, upon your arrival in this city?

Answer—They took us off the cars between guards stationed on each side; marched us through the streets to Camp McManamee, and circling around to the front of the Post Office, where we were detained for an hour and a half or two hours, subjected to the jeers of the bystanders, and then we were marched up into the cells.

Question by Mr. FERRIS—

To what political party do you belong?

Answer—I am a Democrat.

Question by Mr. FERRIS—

Do you know whether any affidavit was ever filed against you?

Answer—I do not. I was arrested, so far as I know, without any warrant.

Question by Mr. MORGAN—

Was you in the court-house when they were preparing to make the draft, and if so, how far were you from the box?

Answer—I was in the house, about five feet from the box.

Question by Mr. MORGAN—

Had you ever spoken to any person about resisting the draft?

Answer—Not to my recollection.

Question by Mr. MORGAN—

State what you heard Williams say about resisting the draft?

Answer—He said he was enrolled in the wrong township, and if he was drafted he would not stand by it, and the officer told him he would try and fix it all right.

Question by Mr. HOWARD—

Had any drafting been done at the time the box was mashed?

Answer—No, sir.

Question by Mr. HOWARD—

How many persons were present at the drafting?

Answer—I judge there were present about forty or fifty persons.

Question by Mr. HOWARD—

Was Williams drunk or sober?

Answer—I judged from his appearance that he was drunk.

Question by Mr. HOWARD—

State whether or not the box was instantly mashed, and so that no one could interfere to prevent it?

Answer—It was done so quick that I hardly knew it. I don't think any one could have interfered to prevent it.

F. M. TAUGHINBAUGH.

ELIHU LYON SWORN.

Examined by Mr. LASSELLE—

Answer—My name is Elihu Lyon; I am twenty-nine years of age; by occupation a farmer. I reside in Blackford county, and have resided there over eleven years. I have a family—a wife.

I was arrested at my home, about ten miles east of Hartford City, after midnight of the 9th of October last, by a file of soldiers, taken to Hartford City, and from there to Indianapolis. From the time we left Hartford City, which was about 6 o'clock in the morning of the 10th of October, we were allowed nothing to eat until we arrived at Muncietown, at about 6 o'clock in the evening of the same day, when we were allowed a mere bite of bread and cheese. We received nothing else to eat until the next day at 3 o'clock in the afternoon. This was on Saturday, and on Sunday, about noon, a light lunch was served up for us, and in the evening a supper. During our entire confinement in the Bastile, our meals were not only very irregularly served, but decidedly bad and unfit to eat, and often missed entirely. Our treatment in this respect was decidedly mean and disgraceful. On our way to this city we were not permitted to converse with each other, or with any person.

The charge alleged against me, as I learned after my arrest, was that I had aided in resisting the draft. The charge was wholly untrue. I never did any thing of the kind. I knew of no secret or other organization to resist the draft in Blackford county, or elsewhere, nor do I believe there was any.

I have heard read the statements of Messrs. Brickley, Taughinbaugh, and Tarr, and I fully corroborate their testimony as to our incarceration in the Post Office Bastile, our treatment while in custody, and our release, having been confined in the same cell, and released in the same manner, at the same time, and by the same person.

The cell in which we were confined, for the greater period of our imprisonment, was a room with an iron-grated door, no side windows, and a tight sky-light. Its entire ventillation was through the barred doors. The room is unhealthy and unfit for the confinement of persons.

I was in the court-room at the time the draft-box was mashed up, but did not participate in the exercises. Politically, I am a Democrat. I know of no Republican who was arrested. In common with those I have named, I frequently insisted upon an examination and trial, but we received none; and when discharged, it was without trial or examination of any kind whatever. During my confinement in prison I took the measles, and was discharged while sick of that disease. It is my belief that the disease was contracted by using bedclothes which had been used in the military hospital and brought from there to us. I do not know by whose authority I was arrested, but I understood it was by that of Colonel Thomas Browne, of Winchester.

Question by Mr. Morgan—

Where were you when the draft-box was mashed?

Answer—I was in the court room, some twenty-five or thirty feet from the box.

Question by Mr. Morgan—

Did you ever make a written application for release?

Answer—I did not.

Question by Mr. Morgan—

In what way did you make applications for a trial?

Answer—To the officers and soldiers who came to the room we were in.

Question by Mr. Morgan—

What answer did they make?

Answer—Some of them said we should have a trial as soon as the rest were brought down.

Question by Mr. Baker—

Was there any cheering in the house at the time the draft-box was mashed?

Answer—I do not think there was any.

Question by Mr. Morgan—

Had you any conversation prior to the draft, with any person, about resisting the draft?

Answer—I had not.

Question by Mr. Ferris—

Was there any disturbance, or attempt at disturbance, with the exception of that of Williams?

Answer—There was none that I know of.

ELIHU LYON.

WILLIAM ARMSTRONG SWORN.

Examined by Mr. Shoaff—

Answer—My name is William Armstrong. I am nearly sixty-three years of age. I reside in Blackford county, and have resided there nearly nine years. My family at home now consists of myself and wife only.

I was arrested on the day of the election, by a file of three soldiers, under the command of Captain Stretch, of Grant county, and brought to this city, where I was placed in the Bastile of the Post Office. At the same time John Miller, Daniel Watson, Thomas Longfellow, John Vanhorn, John Daugherty, Thomas Daugherty, Jacob Clapper, Henry Snider, Gilbert Townsend, jr., William T. Schull, and Bluford Mills, were also arrested and brought down with me. We remained in prison a little over four weeks, except Snider and Clapper, who were released the next morning after our arrival in this city. We had no trial, no examination. John, Colonel Rose's porter, announced to us the fact that we were discharged. Our treatment while in prison was very bad, the food furnished us was not fit to eat; the meat was tainted and smelled badly; the bed clothing was wholly insufficient, and the room unheated. I was taken sick in prison from the cold and exposure, and have been sick since my return home, in consequence. My hearing and sight have both been affected by it. My right ear is now entirely deaf. For two months after I returned home I was under the treatment of a physician for disease contracted in prison. I know of no charges made against me. Those who arrested me replied to my inquiries as to the cause of my arrest, that they did not know. I am a full-blooded Democrat; voted that ticket for about forty years; never voted any other ticket, and never intend to. While here, we employed Colonel Steele as our attorney, to assist in procuring our release. He informed me that he had seen the affidavits; that there was nothing against me; but that he could not get me released. All of us, but Mr. Schull, were confined in the same room for a portion of the time. After about three weeks I was very well treated, but the rest were not.

WM. ARMSTRONG.

THOMAS DAUGHERTY SWORN.

Examined by Mr. Brown—

Answer—My name is Thomas Daugherty. I am twenty years of age. I have no family. I reside in Blackford county, and have resided there for about fourteen years. I am a farmer by occupation. I was arrested at Hartford City, on the day before the election in October last, by Captain Stretch and a file of cavalry, and conveyed to the Bastile, in Indianapolis, in company with John Daugherty, William Armstrong, John Miller, John Vanhorn, Daniel Watson, Thomas Longfellow, Bluford Mills, Jacob Clapper and Henry Snider. We arrived in this city on the evening of the 17th of October. While in prison we insisted upon a trial and examination, but failed to obtain one. As to our treatment while in prison here, I have heard read the testimony of Mr. Armstrong, and I concur in his statements. We paid our own expenses home. I contracted disease from my confinement, and returned home sick and was confined to my room for over four weeks, and have not done a day's work since then. There was altogether some seventeen or eighteen men from our county arrested and imprisoned here from Blackford county, in this matter. I know of no charges made against me—never saw any affidavit. Colonel Steele told me that he had seen the affidavits, but there was nothing against me. Politically, I am a Democrat.

Question by Mr. Baker—

Were you in the court house at the time the draft-box was mashed, and if so, how far distant from the draft-box.

Answer—Yes, sir; about six feet off, and saw Williams kick it, then pick it up and throw it on the floor.

Question by Mr. Morgan—

Had you any conversation with any one prior to the draft, in regard to resisting the draft?

Answer—No sir. The only man I heard say any thing was Williams, who said that he was enrolled in the wrong township, and that if they did not right it he would.

Question by Mr. Ferris—

Was you in the room from the time the preparations for the draft commenced until the box was mashed?

Answer—I was.

Question by Mr. Ferris—

Was there at any time the least disposition to disturb the draft, except that shown by Williams?

Answer—Not that I know of.

THOMAS DAUGHERTY.

JOHN M. VANHORN SWORN.

Examined by Mr. Lasselle—

Answer—My name is John M. Vanhorn; I am twenty-six yeasr of age; by occupation a farmer; reside in Blackford county, and have resided in that neighborhood for over fifteen years. I have a family—wife and one child.

I was arrested on the day before the last October election, at Hartford City, by Captain James A. Stretch, of Grant county. There were some four or five of us arrested at the same time. One of them asked him what we were arrested for, and he answered that we were arrested for "*disloyalty.*" Hearing this, I asked him no questions. On the 16th of October we were taken to Indianapolis, and there imprisoned in the Bastile of the Post Office Building, as I understood, under the charge of D. G. Rose, United States Marshal. I was confined in the Bastile about four weeks. As to our treatment while in prison, I entirely concur in the statements made in testimony by Mr. Armstrong. I was discharged without trial and without examination. Politically, I am a Democrat. I employed an attorney, and through him demanded a trial.

Question by Mr. Morgan—

Was you in the court house when the box was mashed?

Answer—I was. I suppose I stood some fifteen feet distant.

Question by Mr. Morgan—

Had you ever, prior to the draft, any conversation about resisting it?

Answer—I had not.

Question by Mr. Morgan—

Was there any cheerings or demonstrations of satisfaction when the box was destroyed?

Answer—No, sir; there was not.

J. M. VANHORN.

JOHN McMANAMON SWORN.

Examined by Mr. Hanna—

Answer—My name is John McManamon. I am about forty-six or forty-seven years of age; my occupation is that of a farmer and a laborer. I have a family—a wife and five children. I reside in Hartford City, and have resided there for the past seven years.

I was arrested at my home on the night of the 8th of October last, by Colonel Browne and a file of seven soldiers, and was taken to the hotel, where Browne told me I had been arrested upon a charge of resisting the draft. From Hartford City I was taken to Indianapolis, in company with Messrs. Brickley, Taughinbaugh, Lyons, Tarr, and Garrett, and there imprisoned in the Post Office Building. I concur with the Blackford county witnesses, who have testified here as to our treatment on the road to this place, and while in durance here. I was imprisoned with those I have named as coming with me as prisoners, and received the same vile treatment while in prison.

I was present a part of the time while the drafting was going on, but did nothing to impede or resist its progress. The charge upon which I was arrested was false. I know of no organization, secret or other, in Blackford county or elsewhere, nor do I believe there was any such designed to resist the draft. I was released after an imprisonment of about ten weeks. The manner of my discharge was this: The Deputy Marshall, Bigelow, I believe, came to the cell door, and calling my name, told me to "go down." I passed down stairs, and seeing Colonel Steele, he informed me that I was discharged; and I left for home.

My health was seriously impaired by the exposure and hardships of my arrest and confinement. Since I returned home, I have sometimes been confined to my room by illness contracted during this imprisonment. The clothes I had on, when arrested, were light, and no protection against the cold aad exposure of confinement, in an unheated, illy ventilated cell, where we had to sleep upon the floor, with none, or scant and insufficient covering.

I have stated that I was present at the draft. I should not have been there but for the fact that Isaac Goodin, the Drafting Commissioner, requested me to be there, as he desired to speak with me. Goodin afterward said to me that he knew I was innocent; but Dr. Good, a leading and prominent Republican of that place, said that the trouble with me was, that I was too strong a party man. I am a Democrat. I requested a trial at Hartford City, and while in prison here. My application here was to the Deputy Marshal, personally. I had no trial.

Question by Mr. Morgan—

Did you hear any conversation about resisting the draft?

Answer—No, sir.

Question by Mr. Morgan—

Did you hear any demonstrations of gratification when the draft-box was mashed?

Answer—No. I saw some men laughing. I saw none crying.

Question by Mr. Ferris—

What, if any, seemed to be the difficulty or misunderstanding, when preparing for the draft, as to what person was authorized to do the drafting, and what was said in reference to that matter?

Answer—Some of them claimed that the sheriff was entitled to do it, and the Commissioner and Provost Marshal claimed it as their right. Some of them talking, said that they had no confidence in the Provost Marshal, and desired that the sheriff should do it; and when this remark was made, the exclamation, "that's right," was made by the bystanders.

JOHN McMANAMON.

WILLIAM T. SCHULL SWORN.

Examined by Mr. Ferris—

Answer—My name is William T. Schull. I am near forty-five years of age; a practicing physician, and reside in Blackford county; resided there eighteen years; have a family, wife and seven children. I was arrested at the polls in Harrison township at the election last October, by a couple of cavalry men, who, after notifying me of my arrest, gave me until ten o'clock the next day to appear at Hartford City, and from there I came here under a pledge made to Captain Stretch for my appearance here. I came here unguarded, though Captain Stretch came with me in the same car upon the same train. Upon my arrival here I was allowed to stop at the Palmer House until Saturday, when I was ordered to appear before Colonel Rose, which I did. Captain Stretch, as he had previously promised he would do, represented to Colonel Rose that the affidavits against me were gotten up through malicious designs. Then Rose examined the papers, and upon doing so remarked that there was nothing in them, and I was discharged. One of the affidavits filed against me was made, as I am informed, by William Twible, and the other by Stephen Spaulding, both Republicans. Twible is a personal enemy of mine. One of these affidavits charged that I had said "good for that," when informed of the breaking up of the draft; the other charged me with having said that there was no law for drafting; that "I wouldn't go if I was drafted," and that this Administration was bankrupting the treasury of the United States. I was not present at the time of the draft. I am a Democrat. Those who filed the affidavits against me are Republicans.

Question by Mr. Morgan—

Were you ever put in prison?

Answer—No, sir.

W. T. SCHULL.

LEANDER TARR SWORN.

Examined by Mr. Shoaff—

Answer—My name is Leander Tarr. I am thirty-five years of age; a farmer; and reside in Blackford county, Indiana; have resided there most of the time (perhaps with the exception of a month or six weeks) for fourteen years. I have a family—a wife and eight children.

I was arrested on the 9th of October, at Hartford City, by an officer and file of soldiers, who asked me my name, and said they had an order for my arrest. I was then taken to a hotel in the place, and delivered up to an officer, said to be Colonel Williams, who told me he would deliver me over to an officer said to be Colonel Browne, and did so. I was then conveyed to Indianapolis by a file of soldiers, in company with Messrs. Brickley, Taughinbaugh, McManamon, Lyon, and John P. Garrett. The charge against me, as I learned from the officer, was, that I had aided in resisting the draft. The charge was false and unfounded. I did nothing of the kind. I know of no secret or other organization to resist the draft, nor do I believe there was any. I have heard read the statements of Messrs. Brickley and Taughinbaugh, before this Committee, and I corroborate their testimony fully as to our incarceration in the Bastile; our treatment while in custody, and release;

having been imprisoned with them in the same cell, released in the same manner, at the same time, and by the same person.

I saw the draft-box mashed. Williams was the only man I saw engaged in it. I saw the sheriff have Williams out of doors, endeavoring to persuade him to desist from his purpose to mash the box. In the melee, I caught Williams and aided in preventing him from striking the Provost Marshal.

In politics, I am a Democrat, and so are all who were arrested, to my knowledge, in Blackford county. I know of no Republicans who have been arrested.

My health was seriously affected by my imprisonment, so much so, that I have been physically unable to do a day's work since my release. We employed, first, Colonel Asberry Steele, and afterward Judge Roache, as our attorneys, who both reported to us that they could procure for us no examination; that the affidavits had been sent to Washington City. I never saw the affidavits against me.

The Arrest and Death of Bluford Mills.

Leander Tarr examined—

My brother-in-law, Bluford Mills, was arrested, as I am informed and believe, on the day before the election by Captain Stretch, and brought to Indianapolis, placed in the cell with me for one evening, when he was placed in another cell. While he was in prison he became very unwell, and continued so after his release and return home. I often visited him while he was in prison, though my requests to do so were refused for a week or more before the privilege was granted me. His illness continuing from the period of his imprisonment, he died on or about the 16th of December last, as I am informed and believe, from disease contracted while in prison—or at least, that his exposure in prison was a cause of hastening his death.

LEANDER TARR.

THOMAS S. LONGFELLOW SWORN.

Examined by Mr. GIVEN—

Answer—My name is Thomas Longfellow. I am forty-nine years of age; reside in Blackford county, and have resided there about twelve months. I formerly resided for thirty-six years in Henry county, in this State. I was born in Franklin county. I have a family—wife and six children. I was arrested on the day after the election in October last, at Hartford City, by Captain Stretch, and brought to this city and incarcerated in the Post Office Building. As to our imprisonment, treatment there, &c., I fully concur in the testimony furnished by Mr. Armstrong. I had no examination, no trial, and was discharged as arrested without ceremony. Politically, I am a Democrat. After my return home, I was confined to my bed with sickness for some five weeks. My physician, who attended me in my illness, assures me that either the food or drink I used during my imprisonment was poisoned; that my disease indicated the presence and action of poison. I never saw any affidavit against me.

Re-examination by Mr. FERRIS—

Answer—I was present when the box was broken up. When the box was mashed by Williams, the Provost Marshal (William Frash) jumped out of the window, and said: "Gentlemen, I resigns mine office. I want you all to know that I resigns my office. I'd rather than five hundred dollars I'd had nothing to do mit it." The Commissioner ran out of the east door for home.

THOMAS S. LONGFELLOW.

DANIEL WATSON SWORN.

Examined by Mr. HOWARD—

Answer—My name is Daniel Watson. I am forty-two years of of age; reside in Blackford county, and have resided there for about twenty-five years. I have a family—a wife and seven children. My mother and my mother-in-law also live with me.

I was arrested at Hartford City, on or about the 13th day of

October last—the day before the election, by Captain Stretch, and brought to this city, where I was incarcerated in the Bastile. I remained in prison over four weeks; was arrested on the 13th of October, and released, without examination, trial, or ceremony, on the 15th day of November. As to treatment, accommodations, food, &c., I concur in the testimony of Armstrong. I am a Democrat, politically, morally, religiously, and physically.

DANIEL WATSON.

JACOB CLAPPER SWORN.

Examined by Mr. Ferris—

Answer—My name is Jacob Clapper. I am nearly forty-four years of age; by occupation a farmer; reside in Blackford county; resided there about twenty years; have a family—a wife and five children.

I was arrested at Hartford City, on the day before the election, in October last, by Captain Stretch, and brought to this city. Colonel Steele we employed and brought along. He procured my release on the following day after my arrival here. I was never told, and I never asked the cause of my arrest. I was present in the court room at the time the box was mashed, but took no part in the ceremony. It was done by one Williams, and so instantaneously that I do not hesitate to say it was impossible for any one to have prevented it unless with notice beforehand of his purpose to do it. Politically, I am a Democrat. I was not imprisoned while here. I do not know that I was arrested upon any warrant; none was read or stated to me.

Question by Mr. Gregory—

When Williams mashed the draft-box how was the act received or treated by those in the court house?

Answer—The crowd then rushed out of the court house to get out of the way. It was but a very few minutes until they were most all out of the house.

Question by Mr. Gregory—

Did you, or did you see any one attempt to prevent Williams from mashing the box, or to arrest him afterward?

Answer—I did not; he is physically a very strong man; not sober at the time, in my opinion. I did see Michael Daugherty and others try to prevent him from striking the Marshal.

Question by Mr. Gregory—

Did you vote before you left Blackford county?

Answer—I was under bonds at the time, and did not leave for Indianapolis until Thursday after my arrest. I did vote.

Question by Mr. Gregory—

Did you, after the box was mashed, approve or disapprove of the act?

Answer—I did neither the one way or the other, and I heard no one do either that I recollect.

Question by Mr. Ferris—

Did the Marshal or Commissioner request any aid of the by-standers to preserve the box?

Answer—They did not.

JACOB CLAPPER.

JOHN MILLER SWORN.

Examined by Mr. Shoaff—

Answer—My name is John Miller. I am thirty years of age; by occupation a farmer; reside in Blackford county, and have resided there for about thirteen years. I have a family—a wife and four children. I was arrested in Hartford City on the day before the election in October last by Captain Stretch, and brought to this city, where I was imprisoned in the Bastile of the Post Office Building. There I remained from the 16th of October until the 15th of November last. I was released without examination, trial, or ceremony. As to our imprisonment, denial of examination, accommodations, food, treatment, &c., I concur in the testimony of Mr. Armstrong. In politics, I am a Democrat; never voted any other ticket, and don't think I ever shall. There was no authority or process read or shown to me at the time of my arrest, nor charges stated against me, nor by whose authority I was arrested. Captain Stretch was a cavalry officer in the volunteer service of the United States.

JOHN MILLER.

HENRY SNIDER SWORN.

Examined by Mr. Ferris—

Answer—My name is Henry Snider; I am twenty-nine years of age; by occupation an engineer; reside in Blackford county; have resided there for about fifteen years; I have a family—a wife and two children.

I was arrested at Hartford City, on the day before the last October election, by Captain Stretch, and brought to this city; spent but one night in the Bastile, and was released the following evening. I asked the cause of my arrest, but was not told it; paid my own expenses home. Politically, I am a Democrat. I asked, at the time of my arrest, for the authority therefor, and was answered that they had none; that he had no warrant, but that he had authority to take me to Indianapolis.

HENRY SNIDER.

THE SWITZERLAND COUNTY ARRESTS.

GEORGE H. KYLE SWORN.

Examined by Mr. Brown—

Answer—My name is George H. Kyle; aged forty-five years; by occupation an architect; reside in Vevay, Switzerland county; resided there for twenty-seven years; have a family—a wife and seven children.

I was arrested at Vevay, on or about the fifth day of June last, by a squad of eight armed soldiers, under whose immediate command I do not know, but presume by order of Captain Nicklin; and subsequently, per order of Nicklin, I was put on board the steamer "Storm," after having been permitted to return home, under guard, to change my clothing. At Vevay, through Henry A. Denney, attorney, I made application for examination and trial; but he returned answer to me that "there was no chance." My house was ransacked and searched by forty or fifty armed soldiers in my absence, as I am informed by my wife and daughter. From Vevay I was conveyed to Louisville, Kentucky, and placed in the military prison, where I remained about seven weeks. From others, my friends, I learned that it was required of me by Boyle and Dent that my release depended upon the condition that I would give bond, and take an oath abjuring and denouncing the Democratic doctrine of State's Rights. This oath I refused to take, though I was willing to take an oath to support the Constitution of the United States and that of Indiana.

On the day preceding that of my release, I received a telegraphic dispatch announcing the dangerous illness of my son. I then forwarded to General Boyle this telegraphic dispatch, together with the following note:

"MILITARY PRISON,
"Louisville, Ky.,
"July 23, 1862.

"General BOYLE,

"DEAR SIR:—I would respectfully say to you, that I have been confined in this place for seven weeks without being informed of any charges. I have been made the victim of personal prejudices of men of no character, and those who also deserve the scorn and contempt of all honest and truly loyal men. Such being the case, I would respectfully ask the privilege to vindicate my character from the keeping of such men. Let my accusers come forward and confront me, and if any man of veracity will state that I have done any thing disloyal or detrimental to my country, then I will accept your terms. Until that is done, knowing my innocence, I can not accept any terms which will in future reflect upon myself or family. I am willing to take the oath to support the Constitution of the United States and of my own State; but to acknowledge that I am guilty when I am innocent, I can not, in consideration of myself and that which I owe my family.

"Respectfully,
"GEORGE H. KYLE."

My release was a sort of parol, limited to the 10th of August, in which time I was to file the bond required. I took an oath to support the Constitution of the United States and that of *Kentucky.* I reported on the 10th of August, but was informed that they had no use for me. If there existed any warrant or charge against me upon which I was arrested, I have never been able to ascertain it. I had no examination or trial, though I often demanded and insisted upon the same. I paid my own expenses home, as also on the trip to and from Louisville, when I reported according to the terms of my parol. The food furnished in prison was such that I could not eat it, and I therefore purchased and paid for my own provisions. I am a Democrat.

Question by Mr. BAKER—

Have you not been in the habit of expressing yourself in opposition to the war?

Answer—I have been in the habit of expressing myself against the policy of the war among my friends, but not with a view of embarrassing the Administration in the prosecution of the war.

Question by Mr. BAKER—

Did you not, on a certain occasion, at your own house, in consultation with Captain Thomas T. Wright, express sympathy for the cause of the South, and say that you hoped that Beauregard would drive General Grant, or his army, into or across the Tennessee river?

Answer—I did not. Captain Wright and myself were discussing political measures, in a friendly manner, and in that conversation I maintained the doctrine that the General Government had no warrant, under the Constitution, for coercing a sovereign State of this Union. In answer to me Captain Wright said, I was as bad as any rebel in the South, for that was the doctrine they taught; and I replied, that if entertaining the opinions I expressed as above constituted a rebel, I was proud of being one; that I would have my right arm cut off before I would aid the rebellion in any way; that I was an Indianian, and had always observed its laws, and intended to do so; but that the right to criticise the Administration I could not abandon or give up.

GEO. H. KYLE.

FRANKLIN DUFOUR SWORN.

Examined by Mr. Lasselle—

Answer—My name is Franklin Dufour; aged thirty-nine years; by occupation a river trader; reside at Vevay; born and raised there; have a family—wife and seven children.

I was arrested on or about the 5th of June last, at Vevay, by a file of fifteen or twenty armed soldiers of the Thirteenth Indiana Battery, under command of a sergeant whose name I do not know. Captain Nicklin had command of the company. My arrest was accompanied by volleys of insulting, coarse, and scurrilous language, and a dozen pistols pointed at me. I was then taken to the boat by force, which was the steamer "Storm," then lying at the wharf, and placed on board. I demanded their authority and the cause of my seizure, at the time of my arrest, and was answered that it was none of my business. On board the boat I met Lieutenant Hall, and asked of him the privilege of returning home to change my clothes, as those I had on were wet and uncomfortable. I was not allowed to go home. On board the boat I again demanded, and this time of Captain Nicklin, the cause of my arrest, or his authority for it. His answer was that he was acting under the military authorities of Louisville. At Louisville we were taken to the military prison, and incarcerated in a room with some sixty other prisoners, where I remained some three or four weeks. Our fare in prison was bad, insufficient, and unhealthy. I was released upon giving a peace bond in the penalty of four thousand dollars, and taking an oath with a death penalty. The oath, I think, was administered by Major Harney. I paid my own expenses home. I never had any trial or examination, and never knew what I was arrested for, unless it was because I am a Democrat. I have every reason to believe that Governor Morton ordered my arrest. My impression is that I was arrested for saying that I would vote for no man who would not, in the Legislature, favor the return of Hon. Jesse D. Bright to the United States Senate, and that he had been expelled from his seat by a pack of scoundrels.

Question by Mr. LASSELLE—

What reason had you for believing that Governor Morton ordered or was the cause of your arrest?

Answer—While we were in prison, Mrs. Kyle came on a visit to her husband, and stated to Mr. Kyle that James H. Titus knew who had caused our arrest. Afterward Titus came to Louisville and told Mr. Kyle that Oliver Ormsby, Fred. Courvoisier and Frederick J. Waldo had pointed us out. Others informed me that a letter had been written from Ghent, Kentucky, by one James Robison, of that place, to Governor Morton, stating that certain men in Vevay should be arrested, and that that letter was returned by Morton, with an accompanying slip inclosed to said Ormsby, telling him that if there were such men in Vevay to have them arrested. This information I had from reliable persons.

Question by Mr. BAKER—

State the names of the persons who gave you information of that letter?

Answer—Charles Goldenburg was one; Julius Defour stated that a letter had come there, but did not say where it came from. I understand that Julius Dufour is Provost Marshal of Vevay; and others I do not recollect.

Question by Mr. BAKER—

Did Mr. Goldenburg tell you that he saw the letter?

Answer—He did not.

Question by Mr. BAKER—

Do you know that Governor Morton ordered your arrest?

Answer—I do not.

Question by Mr. BAKER—

What language did the soldiers use to you when they arrested you?

Answer—They denounced me as a d——d son of a b——h, repeating the expression God d——d traitor; and cursed me all the way to the boat.

Question by Mr. BAKER—

How were you treated after going on board the boat?

Answer—We were well treated there.

Question by Mr. BAKER—

Have you opposed the war to suppress the rebellion?

Answer—I have opposed the war upon Constitutional grounds. I have said that there was no Constitutional power to coerce a sovereign State of this Union.

Question by Mr. BAKER—

Had you not said that the South ought to succeed in this rebellion, prior to your arrest?

Answer—I don't think I did.

Question by Mr. BAKER—

Have you aided the rebellion by your sympathy?

Answer—I never have, and don't think any one can aid the rebellion by sympathy.

Question by Mr. BAKER—

What did you say about the battles of the country?

Answer—I said we had got a d——l of a thrashing at Bull Run and Big Bethel.

Question by Mr. BAKER—

Under whose authority were you while in custody at Louisville?

Answer—General Boyle was Military Governor, Colonel Dent was Provost Marshal, and Captain Dillard had command of the military prison.

Question by Mr. GREGORY—

Before you were arrested, did you ever say to any one that the United States could never conquer or put down the rebellion?

Answer—I have, in these words: that war was disunion—final and inevitable; that the Union could never be restored except by peaceable means.

Question by Mr. LASSELLE—

You state, in reply to Mr. Baker, that you opposed the war on Constitutional grounds, was that opposition actively or only in sentiment?

Answer—Only in sentiment. I never rendered the rebellion any aid or service to the amount of one cent. On the contrary, I offered one dollar a-piece to a recruiting officer to get some strong war men there to enlist in the service of the United States. He never called upon me for any money; he never could succeed in getting them. I gave another man a dollar to enlist, which he accepted, but came back the next night.

Question by Mr. Lasselle—

You state that you said that we had received a thrashing at Bull Run. Did you express any gratification over that defeat?

Answer—I did not?

FRANKLIN DEFOUR.

HENRY E. ZOOK SWORN.

Examined by Mr. Lasselle—

Answer—My name is Henry E. Zook; aged about thirty-four years; by occupation a cabinetmaker; reside at Louisville; but at the time of my arrest was a resident of Vevay, and had resided there about fifteen months previous to my arrest. I have a family—a wife and four children.

I was arrested at Vevay, on or about the fourth or fifth of June last, by a file of about twenty or twenty-five armed soldiers, under whose immediate command I do not know. I was taken on board the steamer "Storm," then lying at the wharf, placed on board, and taken to Louisville. On the boat I found that Captain Nicklin was in command of the soldiers. At my arrest I demanded the authority and cause for my arrest, and was answered that it was none of my business. I was taken to Louisville, and placed in the military prison there. The room in which I was confined was about forty-five feet square, and, during my imprisonment, as many as one hundred persons were confined in that room at one time. Of Colonel Dent I also demanded the authority and cause of my arrest and detention, and received no answer. My treatment there was bad. I was sick, and could obtain no medicine. I have never been able to ascertain the cause for my arrest. During my imprisonment my wife came and applied to General Boyle for my release. General Boyle inquired of her where I was born, and upon being told that I was born in Virginia, observed that it was a disgrace for any man to be born there, and if he ever caught me again he would hang me. I was released by Major Harney, who administered to me the oath, and counseled me to "go home and stop talking." I paid my own expenses home. I am a Democrat. I was in prison about four weeks. After my release, on the day of the election, Jessee J. Stepleton, Lieutenant-Colonel of the Indiana Legion at Vevay, stood at the polls and commanded the inspector not to receive my vote, and, by threatening me, prevented me from voting, though I three times attempted to vote, and was legally entitled to vote at that poll. I never had any examination or trial, and never knew for what I was arrested. My family was left destitute by my absence, and were supported by my neighbors until my return. No warrant of arrest was ever shown or read to me.

Cross Examined.

Question by Mr. Morgan—

How long were you in prison?

Answer—Three or four weeks.

Question by Mr. Morgan—

What have you ever said against the Administration, or against the prosecution of the war?

Answer—I said they would never restore the Union by fighting. I also said that if they were agoing to make an Abolition war of it to free the negroes, it would not be much odds if they were whipped. I also said that I believed it would turn to that.

Question by Mr. Lasselle—

Did you ever afford any substantial assistance to the rebels in any shape or form?

Answer—I did not.

Question by Mr. Lasselle—

Did you ever discourage any one from enlisting in the service of the United States, at any time.

Answer—No, sir; I did not.

Question by Mr. LASSELLE—

Have you any belief as to the cause of your arrest?

Answer—No, sir; no further than being a Democrat.

Question by Mr. BAKER—

Were you not in the habit of talking generally against the war?

Answer—I never said any thing in favor of it.

H. E. ZOOK.

JOHN E. KILGORE SWORN.

Questioned by Mr. BROWN—

Answer—My name is John E. Kilgore; aged thirty-eight years; by occupation a farmer; reside in York township, Switzerland county; born and raised in that county; and have a family—a wife and seven children.

I was arrested on the fifth day of July, 1862, near midnight of that day, at my house, by a company of armed men, some of them claiming to be soldiers, and from thence taken to Warsaw, Kentucky, where I was placed in the county jail until the next day, when, upon taking the oath, I was paroled for ten days, by order of Colonel Landrum, in order that I should file my bond. At the expiration of that time I returned, having concluded to decline filing the required bond, and reported to Justice Spencer, who insisted upon my compliance with the terms of my parol, but I refused to do so and returned home. Those who arrested me said they had the authority for my arrest, but I did not demand it, nor did I ever hear or know what, if any, charges they had against me. Politically, I am a Democrat. I never heard of the arrest of any Republican. I was arrested on the same night and by the same men who arrested Schmied and William Scott.

Question by Mr. BAKER—

Did you ever say any thing, prior to your arrest, in opposition to the war to put down the rebellion?

Answer—I did not. I never said any thing to discourage volunteering.

Question by Mr. FERRIS—

Have you had a son in the United States service.

Answer—I had a son, a post-teamster, in the army at Pittsburg Landing.

JOHN E KILGORE.

CHARLES SCHMIED SWORN.

Examined by Mr. Ferris—

Answer—My name is Charles Schmied; aged forty-six years; by occupation a farmer; reside in York township, Switzerland county; was born and raised in that county; have a wife and ten children. I was arrested at my home near midnight on the 5th of July, 1862, by a company of armed men, some of them claiming to be soldiers. From there I was taken in company with John E. Kilgore and William Scott, the other prisoners, to Warsaw, Kentucky, where we were placed in jail until the next day in the evening, when we were taken out, required to give bond and take the oath, or go to Camp Chase. I gave bond in the sum of one thousand dollars, and took an oath to support the Constitution of the United States and that of Indiana, and was released. I inquired as to the charges against me, but ascertained nothing. Colonel Landrum ordered my release. A man called Ab. Flannagan, alias Vallandingham, was in command of the squad at my arrest. The commander of the squad, in answer to my demand, said he had authority therefor, but refused to show or read it to me. After our arrest, the commander of the squad ordered his men that if one of us made the least resistance, to shoot us; and some of the soldiers said they wished we would resist, as they would like to shoot the d——d dogs anyhow. We were released without examination or trial. I have no idea what I was arrested for, unless it was for being a Democrat.

Question by Mr. Baker—

Did any Indiana civil officers have any thing to do with your arrest?

Answer—Not that I know of.

Question by Mr. Ferris—

Name those whom you know were engaged in your arrest, and their politics.

Answer—John Keith, James Howard, James Munn, Moses Carver, and others I do not remember—all claiming to be Republicans, I believe.

Question by Mr. Ferris—

Have you any sons now in the United States army?

Answer—I have one son in that army.

I will add to my testimony, that when I was released, Colonel

Landrum read a paper to me which asserted that I had said that I intended to sell my potatoes to the South, and some thing else I should have said about the soldiers being d——d rogues. I forget whether Landrum said it was sworn to. I never said I intended sell my potatoes to the rebels.

CHARLES SCHMIED.

CHALES GOLDENBURG SWORN.

Examined by Mr. GIVEN—

Answer—My name is Charles Goldenburg. I am fifty years of age; by occupation a mechanic; reside at Vevay, Switzerland county, Indiana; have resided there twenty-five years; and have a family—a wife and three children.

I was arrested at Vevay, on or about the 5th of June last, by a file of two armed soldiers, one named Dickerson, the name of the other I do not know. They belonged to the Thirteenth Indiana Battery. I was taken to the Le-Clerc House, in Vevay, and delivered over to Lieutenant Hall of that battery. I asked no questions at the time of my arrest as to the cause for the same, for the reason that I had heard a similar demand made in another case and no satisfactory answer. I did not think it worth while to ask any questions of that sort. While at the hotel, it was announced to me that my wife was in the adjoining room and desired to see me. Lieutenant Hall replied that I could not leave the room, and if my wife wished to see me, the interview must be in the room in which I was confined. Lieutenant Hall remained present during the interview. After being so detained at the hotel for a short time, Lieutenant Hall ordered me to follow him, and I was taken and delivered over to William Mead, Sheriff of the county, and by him placed in the jail. At the time of my arrest I was a member of the Home Guard; my company was on drill that day, and hearing of my incarceration, headed by Captain Grirard, most of the company rushed to the jail, and protested against my incarceration. The door, for this reason, was not locked. An interview was then had between Lieutenant Hall and Grirard, the result of which was, I was virtually paroled until the arrival of the mail boat, about 5 o'clock, P. M., when I went aboard the boat, where I met Lieutenant Hall, and was then conveyed under guard to Louisville. There I was taken to the headquarters of Colonel Dent, Provost Marshal, and the guard reported to him the fact of my arrest. The Provost Marshal inquired what I had been arrested for, and the guard answered that I was brought there to find that out. Colonel Dent then stated that he had no charges against me whatever. The guard stated to him that I was a member of the Home Guards, to which the Provost Marshal replied, addressing me, "Are you a member of the Indiana Home Guards?" Answering that I was, he said I had taken just as good an oath as he could administer to me; but advised me to go and report to General Boyle. I did report at Boyle's office, and was told to go home, which I did at my own expense. I never saw or heard of any warrant or charge whatever against me. Politically, I am a Democrat, and think for that reason I was arrested.

During the confinement of four of the Vevay prisoners, Kyle, Dufour, Zook, and McMackin, a petition, numerously signed by citizens of Vevay, asking for the speedy examination and trial of the men I have named, was forwarded to Governor Morton, who, so far as I have been able to ascertain, never noticed it in way of answer, nor have I ever heard of his attempting, in this matter, any measure for the protection of citizens of Indiana so kidnapped and carried out of the State. I do not know by whose order I was arrested, if upon any; but Rev. E. W. Burrows, pastor of the M. E. Church at Vevay, and a Republican, in a conversation with me, at Vevay, subsequent to my arrest, cautioned me not to censure or blame any one in Vevay; that he had seen a letter addressed to Governor Morton, from James Robison of Kentucky, and by Morton returned to Vevay, accompanied with a slip or note from Morton himself; that the letter stated that there were certain individuals in Ghent and Vevay who ought to be arrested. Mr. Robinson, who wrote this letter, had resided for a short time at Vevay, and while there, had applied for license to retail liquor, and, as a witness, I testified as to his bad character, and for this, he, as I was informed, resolved upon having revenge upon me. Subsequently he ran away from the town, to avoid prosecution for retailing contrary to law.

Cross Examination.

Question by Mr. Gregory—

Before you were arrested at Vevay, what had you said to some of the citizens of Vevay about the war, and the policy of the same?

Answer—I, from principle, opposed the war, in conversation, on the ground that a war could never restore the Union, and because I did not desire a dissolution of the Union. I never talked to soldiers upon the subject. After my arrest and release, I said of the Emancipation Proclamation, that it made the war an Abolition war; and I oppose the policy of that proclamation.

CHARLES GOLDENBURG.

ARBITRARY ARRESTS IN DIFFERENT COUNTIES.

RICHARD D. SLATER (Dearborn County) SWORN.

Examined by Mr. Hanna—

Answer—My name is Richard D. Slater; I am going on fifty-one years of age; by occupation a cooper; reside at York township, in Dearborn county, Indiana, and have resided in Dearborn county upward of twenty-five years.

On the day after the election, in October last, I was in Lawrenceburg, having gone there in company with a party of drafted men, to see them off to Indianapolis. I had been in the town only about one hour, when I was arrested by Captain David Cheek, of the regular service, who read to me a writ, purporting to have been issued by Colonel Rose, United States Marshal. Upon being so arrested, I desired the liberty of returning home, in order to change my clothing, and offered security in the sum of one hundred thousand dollars, if he desired it, that I should meet him on the train the following morning. This he refused to do, and I was at once placed upon the train for Indianapolis, where we arrived that night. I was then, in custody, taken to the Post Office Building, and delivered over to Mr. Bigelow, Deputy United States Marshal. Afterward in the course of the evening, I was taken to a prison-room and locked up. The next day I was removed from that place to the room in which Dr. Horton and Mr. Reynolds were confined. I remained there some thing over four weeks. I never saw any affidavits that may have been filed against me, though I was informed that affidavits, charging me with me with discouraging enlistments, had been filed. Upon this information derived from my counsel, (Mr. Walpole,) I procured several affidavits, disproving the charge alluded to.

During my imprisonment, I frequently insisted upon a trial and examination. Rose stated to me that I had been arrested upon a charge of discouraging enlistments; that he had no discretion in the premises; that he had telegraphed and written to Washington for instructions, and was awaiting them. I received no trial, no examination, and when released it was in these words, as near as I can recollect. I had been, all the time I was in prison, unwell from a disease of the throat. Rose, addressing me, said, "Richard, how is your throat?" Upon answering that it was some better, he said, "I have no more to do with you; you can go home, or stay here, or go where you please; I have no more to do with you." I then remarked to him that I had no trial, no opportunity to confront the witnesses against me. He replied that he had nothing to do with that. Upon this hint I returned home, and at my own expense.

The assertion that I had discouraged enlistments, in any instance, is false. On the contrary, I had habitually encouraged enlistments, by speeches and money expended for that purpose. One of my counter affidavits, the one signed by Captain Crawford, then a Captain, but now a Chaplain to that regiment, the Eighty-Third, and some twenty-five others, officers and men of the regiment, substantiated the declaration I now make, and proved my services in aiding and encouraging enlistments.

Captain Cheek read to me the order for my arrest, and it contained instructions for him to try and procure more affidavits against me. I am a Democrat.

Question by Mr. Morgan—

Are you opposed to the present Administration?

Answer—*Yes, sir.*

Question by Mr. Morgan—

What did you say in your speech at Dover, in your county, against the present Administration?

Answer—I believed that it was an Abolition Administration, and so said.

Question by Mr. Morgan—

Did you, in that speech, give the Administration *hell* generally?

Answer—I denounced the Administration as an Abolition Ad ministration, as corrupt, in my estimation, in strong terms.

R. D. SLATER.

GEORGE M. LOZIER (Dearborn County) SWORN.

Examined by Mr. Howard—

Answer—My name is George M. Lozier; I am forty-eight years of age; by occupation a farmer; reside in Dearborn county, and have resided there nearly forty-seven years; I have a family—a wife and six children.

I was arrested on the 15th day of August last, at my home, by Captain David Cheek, an officer in the regular army, and one Henry Pierce, who took me first to Lawrenceburg, and afterward I was taken to Indianapolis by a man by the name of Miller, also of the regular service. At Indianapolis I was taken before Governor Morton who said that such business did not belong to his department. I was then taken to the Post Office Building, and, as I am informed, before the Deputy United States Marshal, and released because of the affidavit having been destitute of a seal. The affidavit is as follows:

"State of Indiana,
"Dearborn County.

"Before me, Theodore Gazley, a Notary Public in and for said county, on this fifteenth day of August, 1862, personally came Albert D. Jackson, who being by me duly sworn, made oath that he is a resident of said county of Dearborn, and that on Friday, the eighth day of August, 1862, at said county, one George M. Lozier, a resident of the same county, did attempt to persuade, hinder, and prevent him, the said Albert D. Jackson, from volunteering into the service of the United States, by then and there saying to said Jackson that the bounty and bounty money offered by the United States to volunteers after the war was over would not be worth that much brown paper, and was not worth much now; and that if he had any intention of volunteering, if he, said Jackson, would let him (said Lozier) talk with him a little while, he would not volunteer in the service of the United States in the present war.

"ALBERT JACKSON.

"Sworn to and subscribed before me this fifteenth day of August, 1862.

"THEODORE GAZLEY,
"*Notary Public.*"

The affidavit is not true. Jackson afterward told me that at Lawrenceburg he was detained some four hours and over-persuaded to file that affidavit; that at the time he (Jackson) protested that the statements therein contained were not right; that his persuaders threatened him (Jackson) that if he did not make the affidavit he would be sent to Camp Morton; that he requested them to change that portion of the affidavit that went on to state that I tried to persuade him not to volunteer; and that he thought that was stricken out or changed.

[The above answer, as to what Jackson told Lozier, is objected to by Mr. MORGAN.]

My family were seriously shocked and annoyed by my arrest, and I left them in a high state of excitement. Politically, I am a Democrat. Jackson, who filed the affidavit, was, in 1860, a Lincoln-man. My information is that those who procured Jackson to make the affidavit against me are Republicans.

G. M. LOZIER.

JOHN TATE (JENNINGS COUNTY) SWORN.

Examined by Mr. FERRIS—

Answer—My name is John Tate. I am thirty-four years o age; by occupation a bricklayer; reside in North Vernon, Jennings county, Indiana; resided there about twenty-five years; I have a family—a wife and two children. I was arrested on or about the 22d day of August, 1862, at my house by Walter Lattimore, Samuel Dixon, ex-sheriff, and ——— Leapper, and brought to this city, where I was imprisoned in the Post Office Building by one of the Deputy Marshals. I was confined there until on or about the 13th of October. Lattimore, in reply to my question as to the cause of the arrest, said that it was for making use of "disloyal" language. I know of no affidavits having been filed against me. I several times demanded an examination and trial, but received none. At my release, I was summoned to the Marshal's room, where I was informed that if I would take an oath submitted to me, I would be set at liberty. I took the obligation, which was in these words, to-wit:

"I, John Tate, do solemnly swear that I will support, protect, and defend the Constitution and Government of the United States against all enemies, whether domestic or foreign, and that I will bear true faith, allegiance, and loyalty to the same, any ordinance, resolution, or law of any State, Convention, or Legislature to the contrary notwithstanding, and support the Government in its efforts to crush out the rebellion and restore the Union; and further, that I do this with a full determination, pledge, and purpose, without any mental reservation or evasion whatsoever; and further, that I will faithfully perform all the duties which may be required of me by law. So help me, God.

"JOHN TATE."

"STATE OF INDIANA, }
"MARION COUNTY. } ss.

"Subscribed and sworn to before me this thirteenth day of of October, 1862.

(SEAL.)

"J. S. BIGELOW,
"*Notary Public.*"

I understand that Mr. Bigelow, who administered this oath to me, is Deputy United States Marshal, under Colonel Rose.

As to my treatment while in prison, I do not complain of it up to the time the Blackford county prisoners came in. After that the food was not fit to eat. I paid my own expenses home. I am a Democrat. I never to my knowledge used any language, upon any occasion, I considered "disloyal," unless denouncing Abolitionism may be regarded "disloyal." I saw no warrant or process for my arrest, nor heard of any, and never demanded any. I demanded a trial on several occasions, but never obtained it. I never could ascertain by whose authority I was arrested.

JOHN TATE.

JACOB L. KINTNER (HARRISON COUNTY) SWORN.

Examined by Mr. BROWN—

Answer—My name is Jacob L. Kintner. I am about fifty-six years of age; by occupation a farmer; reside in Boone township,

Harrison county, Indiana, and have resided there over thirty-one years; have a family—wife and four children.

I was arrested on the 25th day of October, 1861, from my residence, at midnight, by a man who called himself Moore, a resident of Jeffersonville, and some twelve armed soldiers and four citizens; the soldiers claiming to be Home Guards. I was taken to the tent of Colonel Hazzard, on the Kentucky side, opposite to West Point, on Salt river. At the time of my arrest, my brother approached Moore, at my request, for his authority for making the arrest. Moore stated that he was chief of Secret Police, by order of Secretary Salmon P. Chase, and exhibited a paper to that effect. The charge upon which they alleged my arrest was that of treason, as declared by Moore, and that I should answer to the same in the city of Louisville. No warrant or authority authorizing said charge of treason was shown me, and the only authority they pretended to have was the paper said Moore had as secret police. The men who arrested me were under the command of Moore. From Colonel Hazzard's tent I was conducted to New Albany, and from thence to the city of Indianapolis, accompanied by Moore and two or three other armed men. Upon my arrival at Indianapolis, I was placed in the custody of Lewis Jordan, Deputy United States Marshal. Jordan informed me that the charge upon which I had been arrested was not a bailable offense; but that I could employ a guard to watch me, and by so doing I could avoid going to prison. Jordan named a guard of one man, whom I paid the sum of two dollars per day. Mr. Jordan told me that price was customary for such service. At the end of ten days I had a trial, before John H. Rea, Commissioner, and was duly acquitted. The evidence against me on trial was that of Moore only, who testified that he had heard me say, when in Colonel Hazzard's tent, under arrest, that I had sold mules into Kentucky. I paid my expenses while here and upon my return home, amounting to three hundred dollars, which was never refunded to me. After my arrival in Indianapolis, Moore filed his affidavit against me, alleging that he believed me guilty of treason, and upon that affidavit I was tried before the Commissioner.

Question by Mr. Ferris—

What is your politics?

Answer—I was a Whig. Since that party broke up, I have acted with the Democratic party. I am not an active partisan; never attend conventions, simply vote.

Question by Mr. FERRIS—

What do you say of the charge made against you?

Answer—It is false. I contributed freely for the relief of the soldiers, and have given the administration a moral support. I neither encouraged nor discouraged enlistments.

CROSS EXAMINATION.

Question by Mr. GREGG—

Was you present when your brother made inquiry of Moore as to the cause of your arrest?

Answer—I was not; and what I have stated upon that point is upon information derived from my brother.

Question by Mr. GREGG—

Did you demand of Moore his authority for your arrest?

Answer—I did. He said he was authorized to arrest me and take me forcibly to Louisville, to answer the charge, but showed me no authority.

Question by Mr. BAKER—

About how many mules did you sell to Mr. Graham?

Answer—I think some twenty-five or thirty mules and horses together.

Question by Mr. BAKER—

Do you know what disposition he made of the mules and horses?

Answer—I do not.

Question by Mr. BAKER—

What arms did the arresting party take and carry away from your house?

Answer—Three shot guns, one rifle, and one pocket pistol.

Question by Mr. BAKER—

Did you ever denounce the war as unconstitutional upon the part of the North?

Answer—I have no recollection of denouncing the war as unconstitutional, but fully indorsed Judge Douglas' Indianapolis speech, and declared myself in favor of the Government.

Question by Mr. BAKER—

Do you know of any secret organization intended to discourage enlistments or resist the draft?

Answer—I do not.

JACOB L. KINTNER.

THOMAS P. COLE (WARRICK COUNTY) SWORN.

Examined by Mr. FERRIS—

Answer—My name is Thomas P. Cole. I am thirty-six years of age; by occupation an engineer; reside at Newburg, in Warrick county; resided there five years; have a family—a wife and four children.

I was arrested on the twentieth of July last, at Newburg, by a file of three armed soldiers; by whose orders I do not know. At the time of my arrest I inquired what they wanted to do with me, and they replied, for me to go to the hospital and they would tell me. I think this was on Sunday morning. They took me up to the hospital, and kept me there until between eight and nine o'clock in the evening, when Ewing Bethell, Dr. McGill, and Rufus Roberts came in, and Captain Bethell demanded to know whether I knew of Solomon Coker, A. J. Hustun, William Brownlee, and Alex. Mefferd aiding the rebels. I told them I knew nothing about it. They then threatened by saying that they had enough against me to hang me, and if I would tell about the men I have named, they would let me go. They detained me at the hospital under guard until Tuesday, when they took me to Evansville and placed me to the county jail, where I was kept about two days, when I was taken from there by two persons—Colonel Bates, of the Home Legion, and another said to be a Deputy United States Marshal—to the Marion county jail, where I am now confined. I do not know what charges have been made against me. A few days before the *raid* upon Newburg, I was employed in running a threshing machine some four or five miles back of the river; hearing that guerrillas were in the neighborhood, that is to say, some four miles south of where I was at work, I left for fear of them and went to Newburg. At Newburg I informed several persons of what I had heard over the river. I had nothing to do with the matter. I never gave any information to the guerrillas, and do not know of any one who did. I understand that there is an indictment against me, but what it is for I do not know. I was not, so far as I know, arrested upon any charge, or upon any warrant. My attorney, Judge McDonald, informs me that my trial has been continued until May. I am a Democrat. I am informed and believe that Bethell, McGill, and Roberts, above alluded to, are Republicans. My treatment at Evansville was good enough; but here it is "pretty rough." I sleep on a mattrass laid upon a rock floor. My eyes have been affected since my imprisonment, but I do not know whether it is because of my imprisonment or not.

CROSS EXAMINED BY MR. GREGORY.

I never demanded the cauee of my arrest before the indictment was found against me. The indictment was found a few days after my arrival here. The Court appointed Judge McDonald to defend me.

THOMAS P. COLE.

THOMAS F. BETHELL (WARRICK COUNTY) SWORN.

Examined by Mr. FERRIS—

Answer—My name is Thomns F. Bethell. I am forty-six years of age. My occupation is a merchant and dealer in produce. I reside in Newburg, Warrick county, Indiana, where I have lived for the last thirteen years. He, Tilman Bethell, was arrested in November, 1861, (I can't give the day of the month,) at Newburg, Indiana. At the time I named, a government boat arrived at the wharf at Newburg, having on board soldiers, armed and concealed. Some persons, in disguise, came on shore to ascertain the whereabouts of Tilman Bethell; afterward the captain commanding the soldiers came to my store and inquired for Tilman, and I pointed him out to the officer, when he approached him and said, you are my prisoner, whereupon he demanded the authority of the officer to arrest him; he was answered by the captain, my uniform is my authority. Tilman then remarked that he had done nothing, and would cheerfully go with him if he could get a speedy trial, and asked the officer if he knew what the charges were alleged against him. The officer replied, I do not know what charges, but I am ordered by General Crittenden to bring you to his headquarters. Tilman and myself then went with the officer on board the boat, the boat was loosed, and took us across the river to where my brother Tilman's trunk was kept. The Captain then ordered a file of soldiers to go and bring Tilman's trunk; they brought it down and was about to break it open, when Tilman remarked he had no objection to their examining the contents of the same, and unlocked it for them; they then examined the trunk, and not finding any thing they seemed to be looking for, they returned it to the house where they got it. The boat then took us to Henderson, Kentucky, where General Crittenden was then stationed, and we went on shore, to the General's headquarters; after an examination of the case, General Crittenden remarked that there had been false representations made to him, and there was no cause for his arrest, and immediately released him. I called upon the General next morning, and asked for the information and from what source came the charges upon which Tilman was arrested. He remarked that it would not be proper to make the expose at that time; afterward a letter came to my hands, written by James Root to A. L. Robinson, which had been forwarded to General Crittenden; the letter stated that the notorious rebel, Tilman Bethell, had just returned from New Orleans, and was circulating Confederate money in Kentucky, and that he was recruiting for the Confederate Army. I believe Tilman was arrested on these charges, which I know were all false, without a shadow of a cause to believe the same. Tilman Bethell is my own brother; in politics, we are both Democrats.

The Mr. James Root and A. L. Robinson, referred to above, are both Abolitionists of the deepest dye. I make a distinction between them and Republicans. I do not know the name of the captain who arrested my brother.

Cross Examined.

Question by Mr. Baker—

How long had your brother been back from New Orleans at the time of his arrest?

Answer—About one month.

Question by Mr. Baker—

Where was your brother's trunk at the time it was examined, as you have stated, or when the soldiers found it?

Answer—At a Mr. Hill's in Kentucky, a friend of my brother, where he was in the habit of going often.

Question by Mr. Baker—

How long was your brother in custody.

Answer—About twelve hours.

Question by Mr. Baker—

Were you present when the trunk was examined?

Answer—I was standing on the boat when they examined the trunk, I could see them on shore.

Question by Mr. Baker—

What have you heard your brother say in regard to the probability of the General Government being able to put down the rebellion?

Answer—I have heard him say, that with his acquaintance with the people of the South, it was his opinion they could never be subdued.

Question by Mr. Baker—

Was Governor Powell present at the conversation you have related with General Crittenden, and if so, what remarks he made about the arrest?

Answer—The Governor expressed his surprise that Government officers would arrest loyal men like my brother, he closed the remark that he thought the General would give him a favorable hearing.

Question by Mr. Baker—

Where does your brother now live?

Answer—He lives in Newburg.

T. F. BETHELL.

Subscribed and sworn to before me, this 12th day of February, 1862.

ED. P. FERRIS,
Acting Chairman.

JOHN W. HURST (Warrick County) SWORN.

Questioned by Mr. Lasselle—

Answer—My name is John W. Hurst. I am thirty-nine years of age; by occupation a house carpenter; reside at Newburg, Warrick county; have resided there over a year. I am a man of family—a wife and five children, dependent on me for their support. I was arrested at Newburg on the night of the 18th of July last. I was arrested by order of Colonel Foster, as I understood, who, at the time of my arrest, upon a demand for the cause of my arrest, stated that he would let me know when I got to Evansville. In taking me down on the wharf-boat on the way to Evansville, repeating the question, Foster added—"I am told that you [meaning this affiant] crossed the river with the rebels to-day." At Evansville I was placed in the county jail. This was on Friday night, and on the following Thursday I was brought to this city, and placed in prison here in the Marion county jail, where I have been confined ever since. Neither at the time of my arrest, nor since, I have ever seen or heard of any warrant against me, nor did I demand any, though I did demand of Colonel Bates, on the way here, and after arrival here of the Deputy Marshal, an examination and trial. I have had none. My attorney, Mr. Colley, informs me that there is a bill of indictment against me, but nothing to sustain it. I am informed that Mr. Hanna, United States District Attorney, admits that he has no evidence to sustain the charge against me. The charge that I "crossed the river with the rebels that day," or that I had any thing to do with the rebels, or knew of their coming, is false. When I was arrested, I was, with other citizens of Newburg, engaged in doing guard duty for the protection of the peace against further outrage. I was armed by Mr. Zaven Hazen, who gave out the arms to the citizens. I was called by Lewis Robinson and requested to give up my gun by Colonel Foster, who, when I gave it up, informed me that he would take care of me also. My request, at my arrest, for the privilege of going home to change my clothes, was denied me, and I was carried away without an opportunity of seeing my family. Politically, I am a Democrat. I think Robinson, who aided in my arrest, is a Republican. I have been sick most of the time since I have been here.

Question by Mr. Morgan—

Has the Grand Jury of the United States District Court found a bill of indictment against you?

Answer—My attorney has informed me so.

Question by Mr. Shoaff—

What is the politics of Mr. Hazen, who furnished you with the musket to go upon guard? and his standing as a man of character?

Answer—He is a Republican; his character is good.

J. W. HURST.

JAMES C. BAIRD (Posey County) SWORN.

Examined by Mr. Ferris—

Answer—My name is James C. Baird. I am about forty years of age, by occupation a farmer and trader; reside at Mount Vernon, Posey county, Indiana; resided there over fourteen years. I have a family—a wife and five children.

I was arrested, at Mount Vernon, about the 21st of January last, at night, by four men belonging to the Fifth Cavalry, commanded by Captain Sea, armed with revolvers. At my arrest, demanding the authority therefor, I was answered that it was none of my business, and I was struck and kicked. They then cursed me, charging that I had threatened some of the soldiers with a load of buckshot for stealing my turkeys. I was taken to Camp Graham, to Captain Sea, who said he was responsible for my arrest. After having been taken from there to Captain Ammon's quarters, I was returned to Captain Sea, who told me that if I would take the oath I would be released. I inquired of him what that oath amounted to, and whether it included Lincoln's abolition proclamation. He answered that it did. This I declined doing. He then ordered me to be tied, which was done. Having been unwell that day, I had eaten neither dinner nor supper, and asking him for some thing to eat, which he denied me. I was compelled that night, a frosty night, to sleep on a pile of straw under a wing or fly of the tent. He refused me any covering, though that was afterward furnished me by another soldier, who, inquiring of Captain Sea who I was, was answered that I was a "Butternut." Remarking that I would "freeze that way" the soldier gave me blankets to cover me, and one of the guards loaned me an overcoat. The next morning my wrists were untied, and I was furnished with breakfast. After breakfast Captain Sea again approached me as to taking the oath; and for the same reason I again declined. I was then taken on horseback on the road to Newburg; but returning to obtain my money, which was in the hands of Captain Sea, again I was asked to take the oath, including the abolition proclamation, which I took, and was released. This was about ten o'clock the next day after my arrest. Politically, I am a Democrat. I demanded an examination and trial of Captain Sea, who told me I could not have it. I was also denied any communication, by message or otherwise, outside of the camps; and while I was under confinement, a file of soldiers returned and searched my house during my absence, as my wife subsequently informed me.

JAMES C. BAIRD.

JAMES S. MILLS (Posey County) SWORN.

Examined by Mr. Given—

Answer—My name is James S. Mills. I am fifty-eight years of age; by occupation a farmer; reside about six miles from Mount Vernon, Posey county, Indiana; have resided in that neighborhood over forty years; have a family—a wife and ten children.

I was arrested at home, on the 31st day of January last, at night, by a file of four armed soldiers. On the day preceding the evening of my arrest, two men, in citizen's dress, who afterward, as soldiers, aided in my arrest, came to my house and commenced in conversation the subject of politics. They denounced the Administration and its Abolition policy, and elicited from me similar observations; remained at my house, took dinner with me, and left. These same men, and two others, were the arresting party. Being so arrested, my arms were tied behind me, and I was conveyed to the camp near Mount Vernon, some six mtles from my home, and there taken to the quarters of Captain Ammon; there I remained for a short time, when I was taken to the Commissary's Department and remained there until the next morning. My step-son, (John A. Bell,) was also arrested with me, and accompanied me. The next morning, upon the order of Captain Ammon, myself and step-son were taken down to the hospital, which was in the Methodist Church, where my step-son remained three days, and myself six days. I was released upon giving bond and taking an oath to support the Constitution of the United States and that of Indiana; support the Administration of Mr. Lincoln, and not to speak disrespectfully of the President. Bell, my step-son, was released upon taking an oath. When I was arrested, on demanding the authority for my arrest, I was answered that I would have to go to camp and see whether they had any authority or not.

Question by Mr. Brown—

What is your politics?

Answer—I am a Democrat.

Question by Mr. Ferris—

What was your treatment while in custody?

Answer—Except being tied, and refusing me the privilege of any communication with my friends, I do not complain of it.

Question by Mr. Baker—

What expression did you make to the two men who took dinner with you in reference to President Lincoln?

Answer—I said it was a pity that Mr. Lincoln's head had not been taken off, and this difficulty would not have occurred. I also said that his Emancipation Proclamation had strengthened the South and divided the North.

Question by Mr. Baker—

Had you not, prior to your arrest, on several occasions said some thing to discourage enlistments?

Answer—I did not, only to my son, to whom I said, "let those volunteer who want to." I had but one son who was old enough. I have three sons-in-law in the army.

Question by Mr. Gregg—

Who administered that oath to you?

Answer—Captain Ammon.

Question by Mr. Gregg—

Had he any other office than that of Captain?

Answer—I do not know.

JAMES S. MILLS.

CALVIN JONES (Spencer County) SWORN.

Examined by Mr. Lasselle.

Answer—My name is Calvin Jones. I am forty-one years of age; reside at Rockport, in Spencer county, Indiana; resided in that county for about thirty-five years; my occupation is that of publishing a newspaper, "The Rockport Democrat." I have a family—a wife and six children.

On or about the night of the 28th of January last, after I had left the office and gone home, a file of soldiers, as I am informed and believe, from Captain Leason's company of cavalry, placed an armed picket, or guard, around my office. A portion of them then passed up stairs into my office, where they demolished or destroyed my cases, type and furniture, except the press, which was situated in the back part of the room. The door was broken open with an axe. Upon my return to the office, a short time after the soldiers left, I found the office in the condition stated. I had the county officers to examine and appraise the damage, which they estimated at five hundred dollars, which, in my judgment, was below the actual loss. In corroboration of what I have stated, as to the persons who destroyed my office, I will add, that I have seen a letter from Captain Lease to Colonel Crooks, of the Home Legion, in which Lease, admits that some of his soldiers were concerned in the mob, and deprecates their action in the premises. My information as to the persons concerned in the mob, and the manner in which the work was effected, I obtain from information from others, as I was not present at the time. The impression is universal, and not disputed in Rockport, that the soldiers did it. The paper I publish, as its name indicates, is Democratic, and I am a Democrat.

Question by Mr. Baker—

Did you ever publish any thing in favor of the rebellion? or discouraging enlistments?

Answer—Not that I know of?

CALVIN JONES.

SAMUEL LOGSDON (Spenccr County) SWORN.

Questioned by Mr. Ferris—

Answer—My name is Samuel Logsdon. I am over forty-two years of age; by occupation a merchant; reside at Taylorsport, in Spencer county, Indiana; have resided in that county twenty-seven years; have a family—wife and five children.

I was arrested about the 1st of January last, at Eureka, in Spencer county, by a Sergeant Major, and an armed force of eight or ten soldiers of the Fifth Cavalry. Don't know his name. In reply to my demand for the ground of my arrest, he said that it was for "treasonable conversation." I was from there taken to "Camp Newburg," before Colonel Graham, who said to me that the Sergeant-Major was authorized to arrest citizens; and the next morning, upon taking an oath in substance to support the Constitution of the United States and that of Indiana, I was released. I was then, and still am, a member of the Home Legion. I am a Douglas Democrat. No warrant or authority for my arrest was shown me.

Question by Mr. BAKER—

What was the substance of the conversation for which you were arrested?

Answer—In controversy with a citizen named Waters, he (Waters) said that the editor of the Cincinnati *Enquirer* was a traitor, and that any man who read the paper was also a traitor; and that Mr. Buchannan should have been shot. To which, among other things, I replied that Lincoln out to be shot for his proclamation.

Question by Mr. BAKER—

State, if you know, what the soldiers who arrested you were engaged at while in your neighborhood?

Answer—They were gathering up soldiers who had left their regiments.

SAMUEL LOGSDON.

WILLIAM McHENRY (PADUCAH, KENTUCKY) SWORN.

Examined by Mr. SHOAFF—

Answer—My name is William McHenry. I am twenty-six years of age; by occupation a steamboat-man; reside at Paducah, Kentucky; but generally on the river.

I was arrested at Evansville, Indiana, on the thirtieth of September last, by a file of six of the provost guard, who took me to the Provost Marshal, who said to the guard, "I don't know any thing about him; I have nothing against him; I will have to send him to jail," which was done. I lay in prison there some two weeks, when I was taken out, and an affidavit was then filed against me. The affidavit alleged, in substance, that in the fall of 1861 the steamer "Samuel Orr" was lying at the wharf, at Paducah, when the rebels made a *raid* on the boat to take possession of her; that at the order of White Fowler, who was at the head of the rebels, I attempted to loose the boat from her moorings; that I (this affiant) was shot twice by a rebel while attempting to do so; that from said wounds I was confined in the Marine Hospital at Paducah. This affidavit was made by one James Hughes. After my appearance at the Provost Marshal's office, I was returned to the jail, and subsequently, on the Thursday following, brought to this prison, where I have been since and am now confined. Mr. Colley, my attorney, informs me that there is no bill of indictment filed against me. In the confusion, which existed on the boat at the time she was taken, I did not know who called to me to loose the boat, and never thought of aiding the rebels in doing so. The name of the rebel who fired upon me is George Alderson. I was in the service of the General Government, on transports, after the steamer difficulty for some months, conveying soldiers up the Tennessee river. I have never aided the rebels by word or deed. I never saw any warrant for my arrest, and never heard of any.

Question by Mr. Morgan—

* * * * * * * * * * * *

I did not loose the line of the boat; they backed her and parted the line.

WILLIAM McHENRY.

HENRY HAUB (Gibson County) SWORN.

Question by Mr. Brown—

State your age, residence, and occupation.

Answer—I am a resident of Haubstadt, Gibson county, Indiana. My age is fifty-two years; am a merchant.

Question by Mr. Brown—

State what you know about any arbitrary arrest made in the State of Indiana.

Answer—I know of none except my own. I can not tell the day of the month when I was arrested, but it was some time in the month of February, 1862; was arrested by the Marshal of the City of Evansville and five other men, and taken to Evansville; was arrested at my home. The officer that arrested me had a warrant from James Blythe, commanding officer of the Indiana Legion. I was charged with breaking up a company of volunteers of one Captain Geolser, who was raising a company of the First Indiana Regiment. I had before this raised a company of Home Guards myself, and was elected captain. I helped Mr. Garvin, a member of the present Legislature, also raise a company for the Sixty-Third Regiment. I have given my support to the Government in all respects, and upon all occasions, in the prosecution of the war. I am a Democrat. Captain Geolser is a Republican. I had a trial the next day after my arrest, and it was ascertained that the evidence was all rumor, and I was released. On being arrested, I gave bond in the sum of five thousand dollars for my appearance.

Question by Mr. Morgan—

Was you ever imprisoned?

Answer—I was not.

Question by Mr. Morgan—

How long were you in custody?

Answer—From four o'clock in the afternoon until eleven o'clock the next day.

Question by Mr. Morgan—

Who do you think caused the arrest?

Answer—I think a letter of Captain Goelser to Philip Culp was the cause of the arrest, and Geolser stated on oath that he believed I was as loyal a man as he was himself, and that he regretted that any thing of the kind had occurred.

HENRY HAUB.

AMOS GREEN (Paris, Illinois,) SWORN.

Examined by Mr. Hanna—

Answer—My name is Amos Green; aged thirty-six years; by profession an attorney at law, and reside at Paris, Illinois.

On the 8th day of August, 1862, I came to Terre Haute, in

this State, on business. While there, I was arrested by Samuel Conner, sheriff of Vigo county, assisted by a man named George H. Purdy, who said he was a constable, and had a company in camp, near Terre Haute. I demanded their authority—told them that if they had a writ from any court of competent authority, I was ready and willing to submit, but was not willing to submit without they had legal authority to make it. They showed me a telegraphic dispatch, purporting to be from Paris, and dated that 8th of August. It was about in these words: "Arrest Amos Green for treason, and have him at the train to go east." It was signed D. L. Philips, by John J. Logan. That was the only authority they showed me. I told sheriff Conner that Logan was an irresponsible man; held no office that I knew of; that he was a personal enemy of mine, in consequence of my being retained as counsel to assist in prosecuting him upon two indictments for felony. Purdy then remarked, that he knew that Logan was a "d——d thief." I protested against their taking me into custody upon that authority, and told them I would hold them responsible.

They arrested me and, at my request, took me to the office of Mr. Voorhees. There Mr. Voorhees prepared a petition for me for a writ of *habeas corpus*, which Judge Claypool granted upon an inspection of the petition. The case came on for hearing. Sheriff Conner made his return to the writ, setting up as his authority for my arrest and detention, the telegraphic dispatch that I have before described. Judge Claypool expressed the opinion that the dispatch constituted no legal authority for the arrest and detention, and the cause was informally laid over until the Tuesday following, and I was discharged upon my promise that I would attend on the Tuesday following, or at an earlier period, if required by the court. About one hour and a half after I had been so discharged, I was again arrested by Sheriff Conner. That time he showed me no dispatch or authority whatever; said he was requested to take me over to Paris upon a special train. I refused to go until I consulted with my counsel, claiming that I was technically in the custody of the court. Sheriff Conner then accompanied me to the Stewart House. I sent for Mr. Voorhees, one of my counsel, who met me there. After consulting with him in regard to what I had better do, whether to submit under protest or to resist, he advised me that I had better submit under protest against its legality, as they had a regiment of soldiers in camp, near the city, and resistance would, perhaps, only involve us in trouble. I was taken by Conner on the 11:20 train, going west, on the Terre Haute, Alton, and St. Louis Railroad. When the train got to Sanford station, on the State line, and stopped, David L. Philips, Marshal for the Southern District of Illinois, and two deputies, came on board the train. I was delivered to them by Sheriff Conner. I demanded of Marshal Philips his authority for arresting me. He told me he did it "by order of the President, backed by six hundred thousand bayonets." I refused to submit to the arrest unless he showed some legal authority or process authorizing it; told him of the proceedings before Judge Claypool upon *habeas corpus*. He said that he had orders to arrest any Judge who granted a writ, or discharged any State prisoner upon the return of a writ of *habeas corpus*. He then showed me a General Order of Secretary Stanton, which then assumed to suspend the writ of *habeas corpus*, and authorized the United States Marshals to arrest all persons who might be guilty of disloyal practices, or discouraging enlistments. I was taken by the Marshal and his deputies to Springfield, Illinois. They refused to permit me to stop at Paris, on our road, to see my family, or to procure necessary clothing to take with me.

We arrived at Springfield on the ninth of August, where I was permitted, under military guard, to remain at a private boarding house by paying my own board. I was compelled to pay my own board or be sent to Camp Butler. I preferred the former. While at Springfield I was given to understand by the United States Marshal that any attempt to procure my release by *habeas corpus*, or employ counsel, would be regarded as an aggravation of the offense. I requested the Marshal and his deputies to inform me what the offense was with which I was charged. Their answers were evasive and indefinite.

I was attacked with flux while detained there, and on Wednes day following they started with me for Washington City. I protested against their taking me until I recovered sufficiently to be able to travel; but I was told that I would have to go, and that I could travel in a sleeping car at night. When we reached Washington City, in consequence of my being sick, and through the kindness of Isaac Keys, Deputy Marshal, I was allowed to go to Willard's Hotel until I could call upon the authorities to try and obtain my discharge. In company with Hon. John P. Usher, then Assistant Secretary of the Interior, and who was my personal friend, I went to the War Department to ascertain the nature and character of the charge on which I had been arrested. Stanton was not in, but we saw Mr. Watson, the Assistant Secretary of War. We inquired of him upon what charges I had been arrested. He said they were not in the habit of disclosing the nature of such charges; said "he would not at that time discharge his grandfather;" but finally told us the whole matter of arrests was referred to the Judge Advocate General, who could summon a Military Board to try the casê, or inquire into it himself. The next morning Mr. Usher and myself called at the office of Major L. C. Turner, Judge Advocate, and upon a statement of the case made to him by Mr. Usher, he said he would discharge me if I would give a bond in the sum of five thousand dollars. I gave the bond, and was thereupon discharged. No specific charges of any kind were shown me, nor could I learn what the nature of them were, except through Mr. Isaac Keys, one of the Deputy Marshals who took me to Washington, who told me the principle charge was, "that I was the author of an article published in the *Democratic Standard*, under the caption, 'Can a Continuannce of the War Restore the Union;' and which article assumed that war was not a rightful remedy for existing troubles, and that the Union could only be restored and perpetuated by an amicable and honorable compromise of existing differences." A copy of the paper containing the article, I was informed, had been filed with the Secretary of War, and an order made for my arrest. I had to pay my board and expenses while detained in Washington City, and my fare home.

Question by Mr. Hanna—

State how long you have known John Logan, upon whose dispatch you were arrested?

Answer—I have known him about six years.

Question by Mr. Hanna—

Do you know his character, in the neighborhood where he resides, for truth and veracity?

Answer—I do.

Question by Mr. Hanna—

Is it good or bad?

Answer—It is notoriously bad. His testimony is considered prejudicial to any case in which he is examined before a jury of the county where he is known.

Question by Mr. Hanna—

State whether he has not several times been indicted for felony?

Answer—He has been indicted for felony three times to my

knowledge, and four or five times for misdemeanors, some of them for malfeasance in office. Two of the indictments were pending against him at the time he sent the dispatch, and has since forfeited his recognizances and left the county.

AMOS GREEN.

WILLIAM H. STEWART (Vigo County) SWORN.

Question by Mr. Hanna—

State your name, age, occupation and place of residence.

Answer—My name is Wm. H. Stewart, my present occupation Mayor of the city of Terre Haute, my age forty-three years, and my residence the city of Terre Haute, Indiana.

Question by Mr. Hanna—

State whether you are acquainted with John J. Logan, of Paris, Illinois.

Answer—I am.

Question by Mr. Hanna—

How long have you known him?

Answer—Ten or fifteen years, and probably longer.

Question by Mr. Hanna—

What is Logan's character for truth and veracity?

Answer—His character, in these respects, is uncommonly bad.

Question by Mr. Hanna—

What do you know of him that makes him bad?

Answer—I have known him for several years to be in the habit of kidnapping or arresting men, without law or warrant, and carrying them from one State to another.

Question by Mr. Hanna—

What was his object in making such arrests?

Answer—He was acting in the character of a constable or policeman, and generally made such arrests on the suspicion that the parties might be fugitives from justice, by whose delivery he might make a fee or obtain a reward.

Question by Mr. Hanna—

What else do you know of him that is bad?

Answer—Nothing except from general report, that he was frequently under arrest or indictment for the above description of acts and others.

Question by Mr. HANNA—

Are you acquainted with Amos Green, of Paris, Edgar county, Illinois?

Answer—I am.

Question by Mr. HANNA—

What is Mr. Green's character and reputation as a citizen and loyal man?

Answer—I have known Mr. Green for three or four years, and never knew, or heard any thing of him, but what was creditable to him as a loyal man and honorable citizen, fulfilling all the duties of life in the most exact and scrupulous manner.

Question by Mr. HANNA—

Do you know any thing of the causes and circumstances of Mr. Green's arrest in the city of Terre Haute, in August, 1862, and, if so, state what you know.

Answer—About the 8th day of August, 1862, I was at the depot, in Terre Haute, when the train from Paris, Illinois, arrived, and was informed by some persons coming over in the train that Amos Green was aboard, and was leaving the country, and that there was a dispatch sent to Terre Haute from Paris to have him arrested. Soon after that the Sheriff of Vigo, or his deputy, showed me the dispatch referred to, and which, it appeared, was signed J. J. Logan, of Paris, Illinois. Soon after I saw Green in the Sheriff's custody, by whom he was taken before Judge Claypool, of the Circuit Court, by whom, I understood, he was discharged on his own recognizances. Afterward I knew nothing personally of the circumstances, except through hearsay, which did not differ from the facts as generally admitted and understood in Terre Haute, in regard to his arrest and re-arrest.

W. H. STEWART.

CALLUM H. BAILEY (VIGO COUNTY) SWORN.

Questioned by Mr. HANNA—

State your name, age, occupation, and place of residence.

Answer—My name is Callum H. Bailey; my age forty-nine years; am at present Recorder of Vigo county, Indiana, and my residence Terre Haute, Indiana.

Question by Mr. HANNA—

State whether you are acquainted with John J. Logan, of Paris, Edgar county, Illinois?

Answer—I am.

Question by Mr. Hanna—

How long have you known him?

Answer—About twenty years, probably longer.

Question by Mr. Hanna—

State whether you are acquainted with his character for truth and veracity.

Answer—I have not known him for the last four or five years as intimately as formerly; but when I did know him, I deemed him a man of very doubtful reputation, and rather a bad character, and think him so still.

Question by Mr. Hanna—

Are you acquainted with Amos Green, of Paris, Edgar county, Illinois?

Answer—I am.

Question by Mr. Hanna—

What is his reputation as a loyal and good citizen?

Answer—From six or seven years' acquaintance with him, I regard him, in all the relations of life, as one of the most upright and exemplary citizens I have ever known, and believe him to be a good and loyal citizen.

Question by Mr. Hanna—

Do you know any thing of his arrest, and the attendant circumstances, in the city of Terre Haute, Indiana, in August, 1862; and, if so, please state what you know?

Answer—I saw and conversed with him in August, 1862, when arrested by, and in the possession of, Samuel Conner, Sheriff of Vigo county, as I understood at the time, in consequence of a telegraphic dispatch from John J. Logan to the Sheriff of Vigo, charging the said Green with the crime of treason. The dispatch, which I saw and read at the time, was signed by John J. Logan, of Paris, Illinois, for and on behalf of some other person, whose name I can not now remember. He was subsequently virtually released from said arrest on a writ of *habeas corpus* by the Hon. Solomon Claypool, Judge of the Vigo Circuit Court, who released him on his own recognizances.

Question by Mr. Hanna—

Was he afterward re-arrested by Sheriff Conner?

Answer—I so understood by common report, but did not see Mr. Green after his first arrest until his return from Washington City.

C. H. BAILEY.

BURWELL H. CORNWELL (Vigo County) SWORN.

Questioned by Mr. Hanna—

State your name, age, occupation, and place of residence.

Answer—My name is Burwell H. Cornwell; am forty-four years of age; am at present in no business, having recently sold out my hardware store; and am a resident of the city of Terre Haute, Vigo county, Indiana.

Question by Mr. Hanna—

State if you are acquainted with John J. Logan, of Paris, Illinois.

Answer—I am not, except by reputation and common report.

Question by Mr. Hanna—

Are you acquainted with Amos Green, of Paris, Edgar county, Illinois?

Answer—I am.

Question by Mr. Hanna—

What is Mr. Green's character and reputation as a loyal man and citizen?

Answer—I have known Mr. Green two or three years, and regard him as a gentleman and good citizen, loyal to the Constitution and the Government, and perfectly reliable in all the relations of life.

Question by Mr. Hanna—

Do you know any thing of Mr. Green's arrest, and the attendant circumstances, in August, 1862, by Samuel Conner, Sheriff of Vigo county?

Answer—I arrived at the clerk's office a minute or so after his trial, and can only say that Mr. Bailey's statement, as read to me, is fully corroborated by all I heard or saw of the matter.

B. H. CORNWELL.

WILLIAM D. LATSHAW (Paris, Illinois,) SWORN.

Examined by Mr. Hanna—

Answer—My name is William D. Latshaw; aged fifty-three years; reside at Paris, Illinois. I am clerk of the Circuit Court of Edgar county, Illinois.

Question by Mr. Hanna—

State what you know of the arrest of Amos Green, Esq., and the circumstances under which it was made?

Answer—About the 8th day of August, 1862, I visited Terre Haute, in conjunction with Mr. Green and Mr. O'Hair, the sheriff of Edgar county, Illinois, for the purpose of transacting business. I was with Mr. Green when he was arrested, and confirm the statements he has made to this Committee concerning his arrest; and I stayed with Mr. Green the most of the time that he was detained in Terre Haute by the officers having him in charge.

Question by Mr. HANNA—

State, Mr. Latshaw, whether you are acquainted with the character of John Logan, upon whose dispatch Mr. Green was arrested?

Answer—I have known John Logan for about twelve years. His character is very bad. From my knowledge of the people of Edgar county, I believe a large majority of the people regard him as a bad and dangerous man. There is on file now in my office several indictments against him, and others pending on change of venue in the Douglas Circuit Court. I know that his testimony has been discredited and ignored by juries of our court.

Question by Mr. HANNA—

State how long have you personally known Amos Green, Esq., and what his character is among his neighbors, as a gentleman and law abiding citizen?

Answer—I have known Mr. Green for about seven years. His character is that of a high-toned and honorable gentleman, and his fidelity to the laws of his country is unimpeached and unimpeachable.

WM. D. LATSHAW.

SOLOMON CLAYPOOL (VIGO COUNTY) SWORN.

Examined by Mr. BROWN—

Answer—My name is Solomon Claypool; age thirty-four years; and reside at Terre Haute, Indiana. About the 8th of August last, a Mr. Green, of Paris, Illinois, made application to me as Judge of the Vigo Circuit Court, for a writ of *habeas corpus*, alleging, among other things, that Samuel Conner, Sheriff of Vigo county, was unlawfully restraining him of his liberty. I granted the writ, and when said sheriff made his return, he returned as his authority for arresting and holding said Green, a telegraphic dispatch, to which was affixed the name of the United States Marshal of Illinois, by one Logan, which dispatch directed the arrest of said Green, for disloyal practices, or some thing to that effect. Upon the hearing of the cause, I informed the parties that there was no reason for the restraint of Green, and that if a decision was pressed, I should make an order discharging him. It was suggested that the matter should be delayed without any decision until further intelligence could be received from Illinois, which was assented to, and agreed upon by the parties, and Green was released from custody upon the agreement that he would report himself at a time appointed, or sooner if required. I was informed on the same day that Green was before me, after being discharged as aforesaid, he (Green) was arrested by the aforesaid sheriff, and taken to Illinois. His case was not again taken up before me.

Question by Mr. LASSELLE—

Were there any other grounds or authority for the arrest of Green, in his case tried by you, than those above mentioned?

Answer—There was none.

Question by Mr. LASSELLE—

Are you acquainted with the general moral character of this Logan mentioned above; and if so, what is it?

Answer—There was a Logan who resided two or three years ago at Terre Haute, and acted, for a while, as police or night watch, whom I knew, and whose general moral character I knew, and that it was very bad. He left Terre Haute, leaving behind him that kind of a reputation: and upon the day that Green was before me as above stated, I was informed, and it was the common understanding of those who were present at the trial, that he, the the last mentioned Logan, was the same person whose name was affixed to said telegraphic dispatch.

SOLOMON CLAYPOOL.

WILLIAM B. McLEAN (VANDERBURG COUNTY) SWORN.

Examined by Mr. GIVEN—

Answer—My name is William B. McLean; aged forty-one years; occupation a clerk in a dry goods establishment; residence at Evansville, Vanderburg county, Indiana; and have resided there over four years. I have a family—a wife and five children.

I was first induced to come to this city by James E. Blythe, General of the Indiana Legion, who, in consideration of vague rumors circulating against my loyalty, advised me to come here and go before Governor Morton, in order to have an examination, Blythe pledged himself, that if I would come he would accompany me; take me to Governor Morton, and secure for me an immediate examination and trial. Upon our arrival, Blythe left me for the purpose, as he asserted, of seeing Governor Morton and procuring for me the promised examination. Up to this period there had been no charges, affidavit, or complaint beyond the mere rumors I have alluded to, made against me, that I know or ever heard of. When Blythe returned he was accompanied by Colonel King, of the Nineteenth Regulars. After introducing Colonel King to me, we all three went to Colonel King's room in the Bates House. At his room Colonel King said to General Blythe—" Well, General Blythe, I suppose this is the man I am to take charge of?" Blythe replied that I was. This was on the 26th day of September, 1861. King then placed me in charge of two Lieutenants, to deliver me to Lieutenant Andrews, officer of the guard that day. I was then taken to the house of the Sheriff of Marion county, and handed over to the custody of Lieutenant Andrews, where I remained two days, when I was removed to a room in the Marion Court House, where I was kept in confinement for six weeks, under guard of a file of soldiers. I repeatedly demanded an examination and trial of the officers of the day on guard, but failed to obtain any, and was summarily released; Lieutenant Gilbert stating to me that he understood that I was a member of the "Home Guard," and that I was willing to take the oath of allegience, and and that if so I would be released upon taking that oath. This I declined doing, asserting my purpose to try the efficacy of a suit of *habeas corpus* for my release. The guard was then discharged, and I was left unguarded and no longer a prisoner, when, voluntarily, I visited a justice's office and took the oath. I never saw or heard of any affidavit, or charges against me. There never was any to the best of my knowledge and belief. Politically, I was an old-line Whig, and up to the time of my arrest had never voted a Democratic ticket as such, though I may have voted for individual Democrats for county officers. General Blythe furnished me with a railroad ticket home. During the period of my confinement the letters I wrote my wife and those I received from her were open or opened to the perusal of Colonel King, and it was only on this condition that I was allowed to send or receive letters from her. I was also forbidden, by an officer of the guard, to have the use of any reading matter, newspaper, &c.

Question by Mr. LASSELLE—

Did you ever demand, or learn from any source, the cause for your arrest?

Answer—I did demand but never learned.

Question by Mr. LASSELLE—

Was any warrant of arrest ever read or stated to you in this case?

Answer—There never was at any time.

Question by Mr. GREGORY—

State what excitement, if any, was created at Evansville, against you before your arrest, and state as near as you can, the cause of that excitement?

Answer—It was reported in Evansville, by one Robert Early and others, that I was a traitor, and engaged in affording aid and comfort to the Southern Confederacy, by furnishing information to said Confederacy, and against the Government of the United States. Whereupon I was credibly informed that the said Early and others were attempting to incite a mob to do me some great bodily harm, and perhaps take my life. In consideration of this excitement, said Blythe and Baker advised and induced me to go to Indianapolis as I have heretofore stated. These rumors against me were unqualifiedly false, and had been investigated by Colonel Jones, Attorney General of Indiana, and General Blythe, and by them pronounced groundless, prior to my arrest or coming here.

Question by Mr. GREGORY—

State before the time you were arrested if you did not send a pistol to some one in Kentucky, who was in sympathy with the rebellion?

Answer—I did not.

Question by Mr. GREGORY—

Did you, prior to your arrest, send a pistol to Kentucky to any one?

Answer—I did, to a cousin of mine, with the written permit by Mr. A. L. Robinson, Surveyor of the Port, at Evansville.

Question by Mr. FERRIS—

Who is this man Early, and what is his politics?

Answer—He is the Deputy Sheriff of Vanderburg county, and a Republican—a violent political partisan.

W. B. McLEAN.

CHARLES E. FREEMAN (Tippecanoe County) SWORN.

Examined by Mr. Lasselle—

State your name, age, residence, and occupation.

Answer—My name is Charles E. Freeman; aged thirty-eight years; reside at Lafayette, Indiana. I am a hotel keeper and a railroad ticket agent.

Question by Mr. Lasselle—

State if you were concerned in making arrests of persons, during last summer, in this State?

Answer—I was, as Deputy United States Marshal, appointed by D. G. Rose.

Question by Mr. Lasselle—

State the names of the persons you arrested; their residence; when and where you arrested them?

Answer—Jacob Hushaw, who resided four or five miles below Attica, in Fountain county. I arrested him at his house, on his farm. Also Samuel Stotsenberger, in Rob-Roy, in the same county, who resided there at that time. Stotsenberger is now dead. Another I arrested about three miles from Lafayette, in Tippecanoe county. I do not recollect his name. I do not know where he resides. Also another was handed over to me, and I brought him to this city, who said he had been in Price's army, in Missouri; and another I had arrested here by the name of E. Lamson, who went by the name of Ed. Seville, who was reported to me, by the Provost Marshal of Louisville, as having cut the telegraph wire between Louisville and Nashville, though it turned out afterward that he was not the man.

Question by Mr. Lasselle—

Had you any written authority for the arrest of these men, or any of them?

Answer—I arrested Jacob Hushaw upon a letter from D. G. Rose, United States Marshal, by Bigelow, his deputy, ordering me to do so. The others that I arrested were arrested upon affidavits filed with me by persons, and when I handed over the prisoners to the Marshal, I also handed over the affidavits.

Question by Mr. Ferris—

Was you regularly appointed Deputy Marshal, and if so, how appointed; and were you ever sworn as such officer?

Answer—My appointment was in these words, to-wit:

"United States Marshal's Office,
"Indianapolis, Indiana, August 14, 1862.

"Mr. Charles E. Freeman:

"Sir:—You are hereby appointed a Special Deputy United States Marshal, to act under the orders of. Secretary Stanton, issued on the 8th day of August, 1862.

"D. G. ROSE,
"*United States Marshal.*"

"In addition to the above, I hereby appoint C. E. Freeman Assistant Provost Marshal for the State of Indiana.

"D. G. ROSE,
"*Provost Marshal for Indiana.*"

I have no positive recollection of having been sworn under this appointment, as I received it by letter.

The arrest of Seville was on a telegraphic order from General Boyle, of Louisville.

Question by Mr. Ferris—

State what was the tenor of the affidavits upon which you made the arrests?

Answer—Treasonable acts and treasonable language.

Question by Mr. Ferris—

What do you mean by treasonable acts and language?

Answer—I mean as I should construe it, the people saying any thing to try to demoralize our Government, calling our Government a d——d old black Abolition Administration; that any one who would enlist to go and fight to free the negro was no better than a d——d negro himself.

Question by Mr. Lasselle—

State by whom these affidavits were handed to you to make the arrests upon.

Answer—A soldier handed me one, but I don't recollect his name. I think one was handed to me by William R. Ellis, clerk of the Court of Tippecanoe county, before whom it was sworn to. One was handed to me by a lawyer in Attica, and the other by whom I do not remember.

Question by Mr. Ferris—

How came you to make these arrests merely upon affidavits without any warrant?

Answer—I considered it my duty to do so by virtue of my appointment.

Question by Mr. Ferris—

Did any of these affidavits charge upon those you arrested with any overt act of treason?

Answer—They did not, to my recollection.

Question by Mr. Ferris—

Were you armed when you made these arrests?

Answer—Except in one instance I was.

Question by Mr. Ferris—

What disposition did you make of the prisoners when you had effected an arrest?

Answer—Some two or three I lodged in jail for safe keeping until the train came, when I brought them to this city to Marshal Rose.

Question by Mr. Morgan—

Had you legal authority for all these arrests?

Answer—I had, sir.

Question by Mr. Lasselle—

You state in the above answer that you had legal authority for making these arrests. Now state whether you had any other authority than that hereinbefore mentioned?

Answer—The affidavits and the appointment from Marshal Rose was all.

C. E. FREEMAN.

HARRIS REYNOLDS (Fountain County) SWORN.

Examined by Mr. Ferris—

Answer—My name is Harris Reynolds; aged forty-two years; reside at Jacksonville, in Fountain county; by occupation a farmer and stock trader; have a family of four minor children dependent upon me for support.

On or about the first of October last, a file of about forty armed soldiers, under the command of Lieutenant-Colonel James McManomy, formed a line in front of my house and searched the premises in quest of me. Having had notice of their coming I was not at my house at the time, though I saw them in file and while searching my house, A guard was stationed and continued around my house for three days, when I gave myself up to the arrest. I learned from Lieutenant-Colonel McManomy that his authority for my arrest was an order from Colonel H. B. Carrington so to do. I was then taken by Lieutenant-Colonel McManomy to Indianapolis, and there delivered into the custody of Colonel D. G. Rose, who conducted me to a room in the Post Office Building, where I was locked in. I remained there for over twenty days.

During my imprisonment at Indianapolis, Colonel Rose exhibited to me an affidavit filed by one R. C. Wilson, (as I remember,) in which it was alleged that in a Democratic speech I had made at Jacksonville, in September last, I had said that before a draft should be enforced in my township I would see every spear of grass in my township dripping in blood rather than to submit to it; that I had been instructed by several citizens of my township to call a meeting at that place for the following Monday, for the purpose of taking into consideration whether we should go into it as an organized body or every fellow for himself; that all citizens, both Democrats and Republicans, were invited to attend the meeting. This is about the substance, as near as I can remember, of Wilson's affidavit, and I here pronounce it unqualifiedly false, and have now the affidavits of a number of the best citizens of the neighborhood of Jacksonville, who heard the speech I did make, directly contradicting the sworn statements of this man Wilson.

His affidavit was the only basis of charges against me that ever came to my knowledge. I often demanded a trial of Colonel Rose, who answered me that he had no authority for giving me a trial; that he had caused my arrest under an order of the War Department, and that he had no discretion in the case, except to report me to the War Department. Having been drafted under the draft order, and while I was yet in prison, a proposition was first made to me that if I would go into the service as a soldier for twelve months, I should be released. This I declined, when a second proposition was made to me to furnish a substitute in lieu of my draft; this proposition also I hesitated to accept, on the ground, and so alleged, that I was innocent of the charge upon which I had been arrested, and that I was entitled to a trial and acquital, and that my having been drafted had nothing to do with my arrest. It was then further intimated that if I did not accept this last proposition, I would be forced into the service and denied the privilege of employing a substitute. Under such circumstances I employed the substitute and was discharged from custody.

I never learned of any other charge or accusation against me than this to which I have alluded. No legal process or warrant in the matter ever came to my knowledge, nor was any examination or trial ever had to my knowledge. The charge against me was without foundation and false.

The propositions to which I have referred came to me through my friend Joseph E. McDonald, Esq., from Governor O. P. Morton, as said McDonald informed me, and as I believe.

H. REYNOLDS.

NEWTON M. BOWEN (Rush County) SWORN.

Examined by Mr. Brown—

Answer—My name is Newton M. Bowen; aged thirty-four years; reside in Ripley township, Rush county, Indiana, and by occupation a farmer.

I was arrested at my residence on or about the tenth of August last, by one George Dilley and twelve others, among whom was Charles Allison, two brothers Thomas, George Kinder, Frederick Blessinger, Robert Woods, another Allison, and others I do not remember. Upon my arrest Dilley said to me that he had heard that I was a disunion man, and desired me to go with him to a Justice of the Peace and take the oath of allegiance, and we started, as I suppose, for the office of Richard Phelps, a Justice of the Peace. After we had gone a short distance they said they would take me to Knightstown, and directed their course for that place. At Knightstown they took me before a Justice of the Peace, who declined having any thing to do with the matter, alleging that he had no jurisdiction in the case. I was then placed in the calaboose for a couple of hours, when I was brought to Indianapolis by John Bell, David Cole, John Porter, Abraham Weaver, Charles Allison, and a man by the name of White. At Indianapolis I was placed in the custody of D. Garland Rose, United

States Marshal, who inquired of Porter and his men for what I had been arrested, when Porter answered that he did not exactly recollect what I had said; but that some four months previously he had heard me say, in substance, that I would stand up for Jeff. Davis while I had blood running in my veins, and run down Lincoln's Administration while I had breath in my body. Weaver stated that a few days previously he had heard me maliciously denounce Lincoln and his Administration. I attempted to correct the statement of Weaver, when Marshal Rose ordered me to sit down and shut my mouth. After this Weaver whispered the remainder of his charges against me to Deputy Marshal Bigelow, who took down the statements in writing, and I was not allowed to hear them. I asked Colonel Rose if the gentlemen who were making their statements against me were sworn, and he answered no, that they were not, but that it made no difference whether they were sworn or not.

I was then placed in the Bastile room of the Post Office Building, and locked up until evening, when I was placed in another room below, where I remained from eight to eleven days in confinement.

At Knightstown and at Indianapolis, both, I demanded examination and trial, but was allowed neither. After the period of confinement mentioned above, Deputy Marshal Bigelow came into my room and told me to get ready—that he would take me to Washington City to Judge Advocate Turner; and that evening I was placed upon the train for that destination. When we had reached within about forty miles of Baltimore, I leaped off the cars, while the train was in motion, and made my escape.

Question by Mr. Brown—

Where did you go after you leaped off the cars, and what did you do?

Answer—I went to Baltimore and worked awhile in a machine shop as a turner, and afterward worked in another machine shop, making patterns for castings. Subsequently I worked in Merrill's gun factory, Merrill being engaged in manufacturing guns for the Government.

Question by Mr. Brown—

Has any attempt been made to arrest you since you came home?

Answer—No, sir.

Question by Mr. Brown—

Was any sworn charges ever made against you?

Answer—No; not to my knowledge. The only charges were those made to Colonel Rose, as I have stated.

Question by Mr. Brown—

Did you ever do any thing to discourage enlistments?

Answer—I did not.

Question by Mr. Brown—

Did you ever do any thing to encourage enlistments?

Answer—I have never attempted to get recruits; but have advised persons to volunteer, and given money to soldiers who had volunteered; and have taken my horse and buggy and conveyed soldiers some ten miles to their place of rendezvous.

Question by Mr. Brown—

Were the statements that you heard made to Colonel Rose against you, true or false?

Answer—They were false.

NEWTON M. BOWEN.

HOBBS D. BOWEN (Rush County) SWORN.

Examined by Mr. Ferris—

Answer—My name is Hobbs D. Bowen; aged sixty-five years; by occupation a farmer; reside in Rush county, and have resided there some twenty years. My son, Newton M. Bowen, was arrested on or about the 14th day of August, at my residence in Rush county, by Captain George Dilley, aided by Charles Allison, Frederick Blessinger, Lon. Allison, Robert Woods, jr., Washington Dongan, and Henry Kinder. These are all whose names I now remember, but there were others, as the arresting party consisted of fourteen men. The arrest was made about daylight of the day I have mentioned. At his arrest, Dilley stated to him that he (Dilley) had the authority of his superior officer for arresting him, and that they wanted my son Newton to go to Carthage in said county, and take the oath. He was then taken to Knightstown; from there to the United States Post Office Prison in Indianapolis, and was afterward placed in transit for Washington City. Upon his arrest, Dilley said they were arresting him for treasonable conversation. He remained in prison in Indianapolis seven or eight days before he was started for Washington City. Through his attorney, Newton made application while at Indianapolis for examination and trial, but never succeeded in obtaining either.

After my son Newton was taken away from Indianapolis, I had an interview with Colonel Rose; and in answer to my inquiry as to whither he had conveyed my son, Colonel Rose answered that that was a secret, and refused to let me know, though he said he had "treated Newton better than Newton had treated him." I afterward learned that Newton had escaped from the custody of Marshal Rose, who had him in his custody on his way to Washington. My son is politically a Democrat. No warrant of arrest was either shown or read to my son at the time of his arrest. So far as I know, he was always loyal to the Constitution and Government of the United States and to the Constitution of this State; nor did he ever discourage enlistments to my knowledge.

Question by Mr. Morgan—

Did your son ever have a trial?

Answer—Not to my knowledge.

HOBBS G. BOWEN.

CHARLES H. CONSTABLE (Clark County, Illinois,) SWORN.

Questioned by Mr. Hanna—

Please state your name, age, place of residence, and occupation.

Answer—Charles H. Constable; age forty-five; place of residence Marshall, Clark county, Illinois. I am at present the Judge of the Fourth Judicial Circuit of the State of Illinois.

Question by Mr. Hanna—

State whether, within the past few weeks, you have been placed under arrest; if so, when; by whom; under what state of circumstances, and all about it.

Answer—I was, on the twelfth day of March, A. D. 1863, while engaged in holding the March Term of the Circuit Court, in and for the county of Clark, and State of Illinois, arrested by Colonel Henry B. Carrington, of the Eighteenth United States Infantry, commanding, as I was informed, at Indianapolis, in the State of Indiana. Colonel Carrington represented himself as acting in pursuance of an order issued to him by General Wright, commanding the Military Division, designated as being ——— and comprising the States of Ohio, Indiana, &c. I was arrested about the hour of eleven o'clock, A. M., just as I stepped down from the judge's seat, in the court house, at Marshall, Clark county, Illinois, immediately after ordering a recess of the court for dinner. The circumstances under which I was arrested I understand to be as follows:—On Sunday morning, being the eighth day of March, I received a note, at my house, from Robert L. Dulaney, Esq., an attorney, requesting my presence at the court house, and stating that some arrests had been made in the county, and it was desired to test the legality of them before me; these, in substance, were the contents of the note. I immediately complied with Mr. Dulaney's request, and, on reaching the court house, learned that my presence was expected at the office of Silas Whitehead, Esq., Police Justice of the Peace of the town of Marshall. I went to Esquire Whitehead's office, where Mr. Dulaney came to me, and stating that it had been proposed to sue out a writ of *habeas corpus* from before me, but that the men (I did not then understand fully who) had been arrested on warrant sued out from before Esquire Whitehead, and that, if I would consent to let the return be made before me as Judge of the Circuit Court, and would hear the case as an examining court upon such return, it would save trouble and time necessary to get out a writ of *habeas corpus*. I consented, as Mr. Dulaney was the counsel for the prisoners and seemed anxious that I should, and stated that as soon as the witnesses could be subpenaed, and the defendants were ready, I would go to the court house and proceed in the trial. Shortly afterward, on being informed that the parties were all ready, I took my seat as judge in said cause, when Andrew J. Smith, Esq., sheriff of the county of Clark, in the State of Illinois, made return of a *capias*, purporting to be issued by Silas Whitehead, Esq., Police Magistrate, as I have stated, on the complaint of Elizabeth Gannon, and charging, as I recollect, that John McFarland had been guilty of kidnapping one James Gannon, and commanding his arrest on such charge or complaint. The *capias* was returned as executed, by arresting and bringing into court the said John McFarland. Said sheriff also filed an affidavit, showing the arrest by him, on view of one Thomas Long on the same charge of kidnapping, he having found him acting with and aiding and abetting said John McFarland. The people of the State of Illinois were represented on said trial by James R. Cunningham, Esq., States' Attorney for the Fourth Judicial Circuit of the State of Illinois, comprising the county of Clark. And the said John McFarland and Thomas Long were in court, and assisted by Robert L. Dulaney, Esq., in making their defence. The parties, on the part of each, expressed their readiness to proceed with the examination, whereupon James Gannon, Elizabeth Gannon, Hugh Scott, John B. King, and perhaps other witnesses, were sworn and examined on the part of the prosecution. It was proven on the part of the people, &c., that John McFarland and Thomas Long, the prisoners, had on the evening of the seventh of March, 1863, arrested, at the town of Livingston, in Clark county, Illinois, James Gannon, saying to him that they intended to take him to Terre Haute, Indiana, and that thence they would take him to Indianapolis in said State—that they claimed that he was a deserter from the army of the United States, and that they were authorized to arrest him as such deserter, and take him to headquarters, which they stated were at Indianapolis, Indiana. It was further proven that said Gannon had enlisted some time in the fall of 1862, in the One Hundred and Thirtieth Regiment of Illinois Volunteers, that he belonged to Company K of said Regiment, commanded by Captain Jacob W. Wilkin. That in January, 1863, the regiment was quartered at or near Memphis, Tennessee. That Gannon, and four others of said regiment, being in ill health, had gone out into the city of Memphis on the ninth day of January, and when in the outskirts of the city, about three-quarters of a mile from camp, but within the pickets of the army, they were set upon by a force of about fifty men, part of Colonel Richardson's command in the army of the so-called Confederate States of America, and captured; that their arms and most of their clothing were taken from them, and they were taken about eighteen miles from Memphis to what was represented as being the headquarters of Colonel Richardson; that on the tenth of January they were paroled by Colonel Richardson, and Gannon's parole was produced and submitted in evidence, it being stated that the others captured with him had a like parole. That they were then sent under guard to Jeff. Thompson's command in Arkansas or Missouri, crossing the river below Memphis at Coles' Point. That by Jeff. Thompson they were sent under guard up the river, and were crossed over from Missouri to Illinois, about sixteen or eighteen miles above Cairo; that they then went to the railroad and passed over it to Olney, Illinois, whence they had made their way on foot to their homes; that Gannon's home was near Livingston, Clark county, Illinois. That he was sick when he got home—and had been sick ever since; that he had not reported his capture and parole to any camp or station of the army. This I recollect as the substance of the proof relied upon and made on the part of the prosecution.

On the part of the defense, and as furnishing authority to the prisoners for their conduct in arresting Gannon, were produced what purported to be the copies of three military orders, made at the headquarters of the military, at Indianapolis, Indiana. The first, as I recollect, was made by Captain Farquhar, commanding at Indianapolis, authorizing Captain Lindsey, of the Fourteenth Regiment Indiana Volunteers, to proceed to the town of Terre Haute, and to seize all property belonging to the United States, and to arrest all deserters from regiments belonging to the army of the United States. On the back of this order, written in a miserable hand, and for what purpose did not appear, was the name of Captain Lindsey and his regiment, &c. The second was an order issued by the Governor of the State of Indiana, as I think, and signed by Laz. Noble, Adjutant-General of the State of Indiana, dated at Indianapolis, detailing John McFarland, a sergeant in some Indiana regiment, to proceed to Terre Haute, in the county of Vigo, and State of Indiana, and to arrest all deserters which he should find in said county of Vigo, and the surrounding counties of the State of Indiana, and directing him report, with persons arrested, to Colonel Simonson, at Indianapolis. The third was a similar order, except in not being by order of the Governor, detailing Thomas Long to proceed to Terre Haute, in the county of Vigo, and to arrest all deserters which he might find in said county of Vigo, or any of the surrounding counties in the State of Indiana, and to report with them to the officer commanding at Indianapolis. This was signed by Laz. Noble, Adjutant-General of the State of Indiana, as I remember. These orders are all described from memory, and are substantially set out, as I believe. The defense also introduced some printed orders, purporting to be orders published by the War Department at Washington, treating of desertion and deserters, and some railroad passes issued to said McFarland and Long.

This was substantially all the evidence adduced before me, both on the part of the people, &c., or prisoners.

It was insisted by the States' Attorney that the evidence brought the case within the provision of section 56, of chapter 5, of the Statutes of the State of Illinois, entitled Criminal Law, which is in the words and figures following:

"Every person who shall forcibly steal, take, or arrest any man, woman, or child, whether white, black, or colored, in this State, and carry him or her into another country, State, or territory, or who shall forcibly take or arrest any person or persons whatsoever, with a design to take him or her out of the State, without having established a claim according to the laws of the United States, shall, upon conviction, be deemed guilty of kidnapping. Every person found guilty of kidnapping, shall be confined in the penitentiary for a term of not less than one year, and not more than seven years, for each person kidnapped or attempted to be kidnapped."

The defense claimed that the evidence showed that the prisoners, under the law in such cases governing, had authority to arrest deserters wherever found, and that the arrest of Gannon, in Clark county, Illinois, by them was legal, and that they should be discharged. After fully considering the matter, I, in discharge of what I believed to be my duty, held the prisoners to answer further to said charge before the Clark Circuit Court, on Thursday, the twelfth day of March, being the tenth judicial day of the March Term, A. D. 1863, of said Circuit Court. The prisoners entered into a recognizance, and were discharged for the time, &c.

Regarding that my opinion and adjudication in the premises, had vacated any arrest that had been made by the prisoners, on being informed that three other men were held under the same asserted authority as Gannon, after my decision made, I advised that they had better be discharged by their guard, whoever they might be, and, as I am informed, they were so released from custody.

On Monday, being the seventh judicial day of the term, I made an order of court directing the Sheriff of Clark county to summon and return, at nine o'clock on Thursday morning, the tenth judicial day of the term, a Grand Jury to inquire into the facts alleged against McFarland and Long. This order was executed by the sheriff by summoning and returning, as a special Grand Jury in and for the body of Clark county, &c., twenty-three men. The return was made on the tenth day of the term, as directed, and, by my order, the jury were, on the opening of the court, at nine o'clock, A. M., sworn and charged, and were out considering of their presentment, when I was arrested. The arrest, of course, stopped all action on my part. I had no right to call in the jury and discharge them, nor could I adjourn the court *sine die*, they being still in consultation, and the term legally not expiring until twelve o'clock on the night of the following Saturday.

The circumstances of my arrest not before stated are, that a military force of from one hundred and eighty to two hundred men or more, under command of Colonel Carrington, were, "with all the pride and circumstance of war," marched into Marshall, where I was holding court, as I have stated, and appeared around the public square, several of the officers coming into the court room and remaining during the morning session. I think Colonel Carrington and some of his officers were present when the Grand Jury were sworn and charged. The soldiers were not marched into town until afterward, as I recollect, say some minutes before ten o'clock. There was no violence, except in the presence of armed troops, evidently brought there for the purpose of overawing the citizens of Illinois, proroguing the court, preventing its action in the case of McFarland and Long, and arresting me, the judge of such court, and carrying me out of my own State, into one to which I owed no allegiance, and to whose jurisdiction I was in no manner amenable.

The object was attained. I was brought, under and by virtue of my arrest, to Indianapolis, in the State of Indiana, where I am still held in durance at this date. I have been casually informed that I am to answer to the charge of harboring and protecting deserters, or some thing of that nature, but when or how I am to be disposed of has not yet been made apparent to me. I was confined in my room at the Bates House, and to the house until Thursday morning, the 19th of March, when, through the kindness and courtesy of (now) General Carrington, which has been uniform and uninterrupted from the time of my arrest, I was paroled within the limits of the city of Indianapolis, under which parol I am now held.

CHARLES H. CONSTABLE.

ROBERT S. SPROULE (Rush County) SWORN.

Examined by Mr. Hanna—

Answer—My name is Robert S. Sproule; am editor and publisher of the Rushville *Jacksonian;* and reside at Rushville, Rush county, Indiana. On or about the tenth day of September last, Lewis B. Offutt, a resident of the State of Kentucky, and at that time sojourning as a guest and visitor with his brother, Sabert S. Offutt, an old and respected citizen of Rush county, was arrested, as I am informed and believe, at the Fair Grounds in said county of Rush, by one H. B. Frisbie, who, as I learn, was formerly a telegraph operator in Kentucky; and, on the next day, Michael M. Cassidy was similarly arrested at the residence of his brother in said county of Rush. Said Michael M. Cassidy had formerly been a resident of Rushville, practiced law there for several years, and was also an acting Justice of the Peace—a gentleman of irreproachable character. At the time of his arrest, he was sojourning with his brother as a visitor, though his home was in the State of Kentucky.

As attorney for Lewis B. Offutt, I had an interview with said Frisbie, at which Frisbie exhibited an order from Major General Lewis Wallace, and so signed by him, the said Wallace, who was then in command at the city of Cincinnati, assuming to authorize him, the said Frisbie, to arrest all persons "suspected of disloyal practices." This order from General Wallace was dated on the eighth day of September, and subsequent to, and in violation of, the following order of the War Department:

"War Department, Washington,
"September 7, 1862.

Instructions to United States Marshals, Military Commandants, Provost Marshals, Police Officers, Sheriffs, &c.

The quota of volunteers, and enrollment of militia, having been completed in the several States, the necessity for stringent enforcement of the orders of the War Department, in respect to volunteering and drafting, no longer exists. Arrests for violation of these orders, and for disloyal practices, will hereafter be made only upon my express warrant, or by the direction of the Military Commander or Governor of the State in which such arrests may be made, and restrictions imposed by those orders are rescinded.

L. C. TURNER,
Judge Advocate."

Frisbie claimed to be a Captain in the United States Army, and was accompanied by one Henry Nesbett, who was, or pretended to be, a Deputy United States Marshal of the District of Kentucky.

For the release of Offutt I procured the issue of a writ of *habeas corpus*, which, after service, was withdrawn in order to avoid its resistance by force threatened by Frisbie. Hearing of the arrest of Mr. Cassidy, I called to see him where he was guarded by one Alonzo Swain, but was refused permission to talk to him by said Swain, who alleged that he had orders to that effect from Frisbie.

Cassidy and Offutt were both conveyed away from Rushville under guard, and, as I subsequently understood, were taken to Cincinnati. As attorney for Offutt, I demanded the charges against him, and was answered by Nesbett that he would swear he was disloyal, but alleged no act of disloyalty.

I saw and conversed with both Cassidy and Offutt, after their release from imprisonment. From both I learned that during their confinement the atempt was made by the satraps of the Administration to procure testimony against them, but failing in this they were finally released without examination and without trial, never having known or heard of any just cause for their arrest and imprisonment.

ROBERT S. SPROULE.

JOHN R. MITCHELL (Rush County) SWORN.

Examined by Mr. Brown—

Answer—My name is John R. Mitchell; reside at Rushville, Indiana; am a Justice of the Peace and an attorney.

On or about the eleventh day of September, 1862, one H. G. Frisbie came to me and handed me a written instrument in these words, as near as I can recollect:

"RUSHVILLE, September 11, 1862.

"Mr. JOHN R. MITCHELL,
"*Provost Marshal, Rush Covnty:*

"You are commanded to arrest Michael M. Cassidy and deliver him forthwith to me at Rushville.
"By order of

"LEW. WALLACE,
"*Major-General.*
"H. D. FRISBIE,
"*Deputy,*"

And requested me to make the arrest of said Cassidy. Upon this order I proceeded to the place where he was then sojourning and made the arrest, delivering said Cassidy over to said Frisbie, who took said Cassidy and another prisoner named Offutt, away in a carriage in the direction of Greensburg. I furnished a conveyance for the same upon the following order:

"GREENSBURG, Ind., 11, 1862.

"JOHN R. MITCHELL,
"*Provost Marshal:*

"Will provide or procure transportation to carry two prisoners and four guards from Rushville to Greensburg.
"By order of

"LEW. WALLACE,
"*Major-General.*
"H. D. FRISBIE,
"*Deputy.*"

Captain Benjamin F. Denning accompanied me to make the arrest of Mr. Cassidy. The above orders composed all the authority I had or know of for making the arrest. I did not regard this order as *legal* authority for such an arrest. I do not know what it requires to constitute military authority for such an arrest.

Frisbie had with him an order purporting to be that of General Lew. Wallace, under which he claimed to be acting. I saw the paper, which, according to my impression, now authorized him to arrrest all disloyal persons, or persons suspected of disloyalty, and signed with the name of Lew. Wallace.

Mr. Cassidy, since several years previously, had resided at Rushville, there practiced law and was also a Justice of the Peace. During this time his character, so far as I know, or ever heard, was that of a good citizen, and a moral, upright gentleman.

Question by Mr. BROWN—

You are a lawyer and a Justice of the Peace, and of course know what constitutes cause for arrest. Now did you as a lawyer and a sworn conservator of law, at the time of making this arrest, feel yourself justified in doing the same in view of your sworn obligations as a lawyer and a Justice of the Peace?

Answer—I do not believe it was good cause for arrest under our statute; but what constitutes a good cause of arrest by military authority I do not know.

Question by Mr. Brown—

Was not General Wallace, at the date of this arrest, in command at the city of Cincinnati, and did you not know that he had no jurisdiction, in any respect or for any purpose, over the soil of Indiana?

Answer—I believe Wallace was in command at Cincinnati at the time. I know nothing of the extent of his jurisdiction.

Question by Mr. Brown—

Did you not know that there was no such office or officer as *Deputy* Major General?

Answer—I never thought any thing about it at the time of the arrest. My understanding now is that there is no such office or officer.

Question by Mr. Brown—

Then you admit that in making the arrest you did so without legal or military authority, and that the "order," so termed, was a sham, and you had no right whatever to make said arrest?

Answer—My impression now is that the arrest was unauthorized, though I did not think so at the time, and I acted in good faith.

Question by Mr. Brown—

What is your politics?

Answer—I have been a Republican.

JOHN R. MITCHELL.

MINORITY REPORT

OF THE

COMMITTEE

ON

ARBITRARY ARRESTS.

MINORITY REPORT.

The Minority of the Committee on Arbitrary Arrests beg leave to make the following report, accompanied with the evidence and Majority Report of said Committee, together with the resolutions of this House on that subject, passed by a strict party vote.

We respectfully dissent from the Majority Report of said Committee, nor can we agree with them in admitting, for one moment, that the arrests complained of in this State were arbitrary, unjust, and illegal, or that they were subversive of the Constitution of the United States or of this State, or dangerous to the liberties of the people; but, upon the contrary, they were strictly made for the protection of the Government—to sustain the rights and privileges of the true and loyal citizens of the nation, and to aid those in authority in crushing out the rebellion and restoring the Union.

As a matter of history, it is well known to the American people that President Lincoln, in the strict line of his constitutional duty, some time last fall published an order in relation to those disloyal practices which were calculated to weaken the arm of the Government and give aid and comfort to the enemy.

Every reading and thinking man well knows the condition of the country at the time that order was published. Our enemies (the rebels) outnumbered us in the field; our army for the restoration of the Union had been greatly thinned by disease and death. We had been virtually repulsed in the seven days' fight before Richmond; we had met with disaster in Kentucky and at other points, and General Buell was after General Bragg's rebel army. The free States were threatened by the invading rebel foe—every thing looked dark and gloomy; for a time the people were in awful suspense as to the fate of the nation and the safety of the heroic band of Union soldiers, who were battling against disease and the armed rebels of the country.

At this time a quick and bold move had to be made by the Commander-in-Chief of the nation, or all would be lost, and that soon —the soldiers in the field would perish with the overthrow of the Government. President Lincoln, with an honest purpose to fulfill his duty, and his whole constitutional duty to the country under his solemn oath of office, as President of the United States, came at once to the rescue by calling out three hundred thousand additional troops; and hearing the low mutterings of treason and of treasonable acts and conduct by those who were disloyal to their Government in many of the loyal States North, he sent forth his order, alluded to, to hush for ever, if possible, that treason which was fast sapping the very vitals and life's blood of the nation.

The President did nothing but his duty under the Constitution. Had he acted differently, he would have been recreant to his high trusts; and had he failed to adopt proper measures for the saving of the soldiers then in the field, and had they perished by his neglect and the Union lost, mankind would have pronounced him even worse than a Buchanan—a fit associate of the traitors Arnold, Burr and Jeff. Davis. He did his duty, and loyal men had nothing to fear, as his orders making the arrests and the suspending of the writ of *habeas corpus* were not intended for them. The loyal are just as safe as they ever were in times of the most profound peace, having a clear conscience, sleep soundly, being at no time in danger unless at the hands of the enemies of the country. Had all in the free States been of this class, and had loyalty been universal over the land, no such orders would have been necessary. But these orders and proclamations of the President are terrible things to traitors, and those who speak and sympathize with them.

The God of Heaven and the Constitution of the United States never gave any citizen the right to say, do, and speak whatever he pleased, without reference to whether it was right or wrong. That Constitution protects the right and punishes the wrong. A man may say all he pleases of his neighbor or his Government, provided he pleases to. This is the light in which the immortal Jackson and the great Democratic party of the country viewed this subject in years past.

General Jackson, being a Major General, subordinate to the President of the United States, after he fought his great battle at New Orleans, made some arbitrary arrests of Louisiana legislators, and among the rest a certain Judge Hall, of the United States Court, some for publications used toward himself as commander, and against Judge Hall for issuing a writ of *habeas corpus* for the release of a certain legislator, whom General Jackson had ordered to be arrested under military law; whereupon General Jackson ordered immediately the arrest of Judge Hall for his judicial act, in issuing the writ of *habeas corpus*, and he was accordingly arrested. Soon peace was declared with Great Britain, and Judge Hall was released by order of General Jackson, and afterward the Judge had the General brought before his Court to answer for his conduct in the matter; was fined by the court one thousand dollars, and in after years every Democrat in Congress voted to refund to General Jackson the said fine, which was done.

Stephen A. Douglas, the great champion of Democracy in his day, advocated the passage of the law refunding to General Jackson, and alleging that Judge Hall did wrong in fining General Jackson at all; and that the arrest of the Judge by General Jackson was right, and the Democratic votes in Congress indorsed the sentiments of Stephen A. Douglas.

Thus was set the great example of suspending the writ of *habeas corpus*, and of making arbitrary arrests, and proclaiming martial law in time of war.

And this example was set by the great apostle of Democracy of his day, and was so approved by his party. Posterity will bless and honor the acts of that great patriot, soldier, and statesman. So will posterity and mankind throughout the civilized world, who love free government and our noble union of States, honor and bless the name of "honest Old Abe" Lincoln for treading in the footsteps of the hero of New Orleans.

If any cause of complaint may exist, we venture to say that the future historian of America, and the readers of the acts of this great rebellion in after times, will wonder with shame and astonishment why it was that this Administration did not, with a more swift vengeance, punish the outlaw and traitor in whatever part of the United States he was found.

From the evidence before the country, we of this time should have no complaint to enter against the President and those executing the laws under him, unless for the mercy exercised by him and his supporters against the rebels and traitors of the land.

As to the constitutional power of the President to suspend the writ of *habeas corpus*, and of making arrests of disloyal persons in time of war, invasion, or rebellion, there can be no doubt. His war power under that instrument makes him the Commander-in-

Chief of the Army and Navy of the United States, and that same Constitution requires that he shall see that the laws of the land are faithfully executed, and that in cases of invasion and insurrection the privilege of the writ of *habeas corpus* may be suspended.

Some say that Congress ought to pass a law on that subject: First, to give the President power to do these things before he can act, and, as a reason, they say the President might act tyrannically if this was not the case. This amounts to no argument whatever, for the reason that the President, if corrupt, could be as tyrannical one way as well as the other.

On that subject the people must, as they always have trusted, continue to trust to the honesty of the President. If in such cases the President abuses his constitutional trusts there are but two ways to remedy the evil; one by impeachment and the other at the ballot-box.

Again, in the *interim* of Congress, the members all being at home, from three to five thousand miles apart, some in the Eastern States, some in the Pacific States, and scattered all over the land. Suddenly the country is invaded, or an insurrection or rebellion breaks out, so great and so cunningly arranged that the insurgents or rebels are able to capture a majority of the members of Congress, what is the President to do? Shall he let the Government go overboard by default? No, sir! He must execute the laws under the Constitution, and in doing so he has the right and power to arrest, imprison, chain or hang every traitor in the land. And this awful penalty should be meted out to all those who give aid and comfort to the same. And to save the Constitution unimpaired, he might, if white agents gave out, employ black agents to kill white traitors.

Right here we may notice another class of constitutional objectors, who declare that in all cases, whether in peace or in war, the military power of the nation must be in subjection to the civil authority.

In time of war the civil authority must only be in subjection to the military *whenever public safety demands it.*

If this was not so, under the Constitution, then there could never be a battle fought against rebels, for the Constitution expressly declares, that no person shall be deprived of life, liberty, or property, without due process of law.

That is, no man shall lose his life, under the Constitution, until a court of competent jurisdiction has heard his or her cause, and found the accused guilty of a crime against the United States worthy of death, and thereupon the court pronounces sentence of death, and the person is executed accordingly. And this same process must be gone through with, in regard to liberty and property: that is, life, liberty, and property, must be taken away by judicial judgment and decree.

Now this is all right, and applies to times of *peace;* but has nothing at all to do with the rights of war under the Constitution. Apply this kind of interpretation to about thirty thousand armed rebels, with guns in their hands, and you will find that judgments of courts are not for their case. The Union army comes in sight of them, and is about to begin to shoot, when some guardian of human liberty, with his hat full of writs of *habeas corpuses*, comes up, and this walking commentary of the Constitution cries, with a loud voice, "stop!"

"Here's work of another kind. In our peculiar form of government, the military must always be in subjection to the civil authority; therefore, call a jury to try these thirty thousand fellows, before you take their life; for that is the only way to get a man's life from him, under our Millennium Constitution."

Thus speak all that class of men who have not been blessed with a sight of that part of the Constitution known as the *military part.* But some wag, at this point, while the jury is being made up, urges another objection, viz: that a man can not be tried, according to the Constitution, for a crime, where his life is at stake, unless he is personally present, and the difficulty that presents itself to the court and jury is, that these thirty thousand fellows won't consent to be *arrested*, for fear the writ of *habeas corpus* will not release them.

Now what is to be done in a case like the one just put? Why, do just what common sense and the Constitution says do, exercise the military power; hurl the army of the country down upon the rebels, and kill every one of them, if they do not surrender.

All such as would, in times of war, make the civil authority supreme and above the military power, were begotten and brought forth by either *ignorance* or *treason*.

And all that class of persons who are constantly talking of the *habeas corpus*, and are very much alarmed for fear its great liberty features will be violated—they need more patriotism—for they are *not* such friends to human liberty as to trust that great boon to their keeping.

The Constitution of the United States is plain on the question of the writ of *habeas corpus*. Just such *times* as are now in the land, *are the exact kind* of *times* when the privileges of that great writ and charter of liberty ought to be suspended. Listen to what it says: "The *privilege* of the writ of *habeas corpus* shall not be suspended unless when, in cases of rebellion or insurrection, the *public safety may require it.*" That is the ring of the true metal. The President suspended its privileges when the *public safety* demanded it, and for it the nation and posterity will thank him.

After the resolutions, passed at the present Legislature, creating this Committee of Arbitrary Arrests, with the powers granted to said Committee, with the evidence accompanying the same, shall have been read and studied by the thousands whose minds it was intended to prejudice against the legally constituted officials of the nation, another grave constitutional question will arise, hard, indeed, to be explained by the partisan leaders who have set themselves up against the policy adopted by this Administration for the overthrow and suppression of the rebellion, which is this: "Can a State Legislature create any power, by the appointment of a Committee, or otherwise, to try the acts and official doings of the President of the United States, the Secretary of War, or the United States Marshal, acting under their authority?" We answer, no. If this be the correct answer, of which we have no doubt, then this Committee derived no such power to act in the premises, and their proceedings are nugatory, costing the State a few thousand dollars for the purpose of creating, if possible, a little political capital against the Government, and those who are its best friends.

The impartial, loyal reader of this and after times, will be fully able, after reading the evidence taken before this Committee, whether Mr. Lincoln had abused the high trusts committed to him, and was thereby attempting to promote himself to the position of a Dictator, by destroying the safeguards of human liberty under the Constitution, or was only honestly and faithfully attempting to sustain the Government in its great struggle with the hundreds of thousands of armed and wicked rebels, and preserve, if possible, the noble and worthy Union Army. That the latter is true of the President, no man can doubt. That some errors may have been committed in this great strife for national existence, on the part of those in power, no one will deny, "for to err is human." The greatest and best men in all ages of the world have had their imperfections, yet at the same time their motives were pure and honest.

So with the President, so with Governor Morton, so with all pure-minded patriots and statesmen, in this strife for liberty and free government. A careful review of the evidence adduced before the Committee, shows that scarcely one was arrested and imprisoned for a short time, but had been engaged in saying or doing some thing calculated to give aid and comfort to the enemy; such as discouraging enlistments of soldiers, resisting the draft in Blackford and Fountain counties, giving countenance to the destruction of the draft-box in Blackford county, where shouts from traitor lips went up for "Jeff. Davis" and the Southern Confederacy. And in other cases the evidence of men taken at the jail in the city of Indianapolis, against whom indictments were pending at the time for treason.

In nearly all the cases where arrests were made, the affidavit of one or more credible, competent, and loyal witnesses were taken and filed against the accused, charging them with disloyalty to the Government; and where there was no affidavit filed, arrests were made by subordinate military officers for the sole good of the cause of the country, not to destroy the last vestige of human liberty, but to preserve the nation.

And here, we may be permitted to say, had the old Democratic doctrine of General Jackson been followed out, which his friends have heretofore sustained, many more arrests would have been made than were made, and more hemp would have been used than was used; which no doubt would have produced better results for the good of the country than were produced. A studied and searching attempt has been made by the political opponents and enemies of Governor Morton, to detract from his great and well-earned fame in his untiring devotion to the cause of his country and the noble State over which he is Governor; but in that his enemies have signally failed; their attempts and efforts in this unholy line of corrupt policy, will stink in the nostrils of every true patriot in the land, while *his* fame for patriotism and love of country will stand unrivaled in the minds and affections of the lovers of liberty and humanity throughout all the civilized free governments.

Would-be leaders of a once great party assume that name ("Democracy") in this rebellion, who have no more right to it, from their conduct toward the Government, than a *wolf* has to wear the fleece of a *sheep.* They struggle hard to make the people believe that they are the only ones left now in the land to advocate free speech and free government, and many have been deceived into their meshes; they have labored so incessantly against the policy of the present Administration, that many have landed in the enemy's camp, and many more are on the road, standing in a stone's throw of the enemy's lines. And this opposition has become so fearful and dangerous, that the ignorant and prejudiced, in many places, have sought homes in hellish secret leagues, that they might more effectually concoct and perfect, under traitor leaders, their infernal schemes of treason and rebellion for the overthrow of the Government; which resistance to the laws and Constitution of the land, if persevered in by them, must bring devastation, war, blood-shed, total anarchy, and ruin all over this once happy and prosperous country. For what? Simply to gratify a few political leaders, who are gasping and grasping for place and power, which they never can attain, but must go down to posterity, disgraced and dishonored by all the true and loyal of the country.

To all such unprincipled, ambitious leaders, the advice might be given, at once change your deadly policy; correct your false teachings to the people; help at once to extinguish the flames of secession and rebellion, and you may yet have some hope left in the great future, if the Government is sustained, for honor, place, and power.

That the right, in this great struggle for free government and free institutions, will triumph, and the Union be perpetuated and maintained, under the benign smiles of an overruling Providence, we have no doubts or fears.

Our political faith looks to a bright future, when the Union Army and Navy shall have triumphed over every opposing foe, whether he be despot or traitor; and the facts will be fully established, that man is capable of self-government, and that, with the increase of intelligence and love of liberty infused into the American mind, no power will be ever able to cope with *our country* in art, science, civilization, or war; and that in the galaxy of American States, Indiana will shine forth in the foremost ranks of them all, for the valor of her soldiers, the patriotism of her people, and the efficiency of her noble Governor.

BENJAMIN F. GREGORY,
JAMES M. GREGG,
CHARLES D. MORGAN,
TIMOTHY BAKER.

EVIDENCE.

ABRAHAM B. JETMORE (Blackford County) SWORN.

Examined by Mr. Gregory—

Answer—My name is Abraham B. Jetmore; aged twenty-four years; residence Hartford City, Blackford county; I am an attorney at law; I have been and am yet a life-long Democrat, when political questions should be agitated; voted for Douglas for President.

On or about the second day of October last, at a Union and War Meeting combined, at a school house in Nottingham township, Wells county, at which one John Phipps went with me for the purpose of raising recruits. After I had delivered my discourse, or the principal portion of it, Dr. Theodore Horton rose and said he wished to speak. I had asked before or after, and perhaps both before and after, the said Phipps (who was recruiting officer for the Thirty-Second Indiana Regiment,) to come forth and ask for volunteers, and he did so. Whereupon Mr. Horton came forth and began his discourse, and used, as near as I can recollect, the following language: "I always knew this (meaning the present) war was an Abolition war. The late proclamation of the President has capped the Abolition climax. You have been called upon to-night to volunteer; but has any of you volunteered? No, not one. You will not volunteer under such a policy." I do not think said Mr. Horton answered over one or two points made in my discourse, he having came at a late hour. I think that he principally heard me in my exhortation for volunteers. I have never had any personal difficulty with Dr. Horton; on the contrary, I voted for him in 1860. I can not particularize any other language he used derogatory to the interests of the Government, but I know he used other. The greater portion of what he said in his said discourse, if believed, would have a tendency to alienate the people from the Government.

Question by Mr. GREGORY—

State whether you was present at Hartford City, in Blackford county, the day the draft was attempted to be made; and, if so, state all you know about it?

Answer—I was in Hartford City that day. In the forenoon of said day, when the citizens began to gather in, there appeared to be an excitement among some of them, and had a tendency to increase, and, in the afternoon, from where I stood across the street, I saw there was considerable indications of a mob; a good many of them having their coats off and sleeves rolled up. When the officers went across to the court house, there was a general rush made after them. After a while, I heard a considerable noise in the court house, stamping and hallooing. Immediately there was a rush made out of doors. Whereupon I was informed the draft-box was mashed.

The persons I saw appearing to be taking sides with the mob were these: One Henry Snider came up before the box was reported to be mashed, and before the rush was made into the house, and took off his coat and laid it in the window, and rolled up his sleeves and rushed in with the rest. I saw Jess. Williams also, with his sleeves rolled up, brandishing his fists; and also John Vanhorn had his coat off and sleeves rolled up; also Leander Tarr; also John Daugherty, I think, and several others whom I can not enumerate. After the rush was made out of the court house, I saw John Vanhorn with a paper in his hand tearing it in shrivers, throwing it to the earth and stamping it. There appeared to be fifteen or twenty taking sides. From the action of the mob there appeared to be concert among them.

Question by Mr. GIVEN—

State if you voted for the Democratic State Ticket at the last election?

Answer—I did not vote the ticket nominated at the 8th of January Convention.

Question by Mr. GIVEN—

State if you voted the Republican State Ticket nominated on the 18th of June, 1862?

Answer—I do not know of any Republican ticket being nominated that day; but I know of a Union ticket being nominated that day.

Question by Mr. GIVEN—

State who were the nominees of this "Union" Convention of which you speak?

Answer—I do not recollect all their names; but they are designated as "Union" men, composed of part Democrats and part Republicans.

Question by Mr. GIVEN—

Did you vote for Shanks, Republican, or McDonell, Democratic candidate for Congress in your Congressional District, at the last election?

Answer—I voted for Shanks "Union" candidate.

Question by Mr. GIVEN—

Was not Shanks, in 1860, elected to Congress, and, if so, by what party?

Answer—By the then Republican party.

Question by Mr. GIVEN—

State if you were a candidate at the late election, and if so, for what office, and nominated by what party?

Answer—I was a candidate for Representative from Blackford and Wells counties; was placed upon the track by the "Union" citizens of said counties.

Question by Mr. GIVEN—

Were you nominated by the Democratic party of Blackford and Wells counties?

Answer—I was not the nominee of the so-called Democratic party.

Question by Mr. GIVEN—

What do you mean by "the Government?"

Answer—I understand the Legislative, the Executive, and Judicial, combined, together with the people.

Question by Mr. GIVEN—

What do you mean by the term "Abolitionist?"

Answered—I term it any person or persons who will use all power, or believe it right, to abolish human slavery against the will of any State or States whose Constitution recognizes the same where it legally, lawfully, and loyally exists.

Question by Mr. GIVEN—

Did you, or did you not, approve of the remarks of Dr. Horton made at that meeting?

Answer—I did not.

Question by Mr. GIVEN—

Do you approve of the Emancipation Proclamation of the President of September last, denounced by Dr. Horton?

Answer—As Commander-in-Chief of the Army I do; but would not as Civil Executive.

Question by Mr. Shoaff—

Do you then understand that the "Civil Executive" has vacated his seat?

Answer—I do not; but, on the contrary, I consider the President has two-fold power: First, Civil Executive; secondly, Commander-in-Chief.

Question by Mr. Given—

State what part, if any, you took in the arrest of Dr. Horton?

Answer—I took no part. I filed an affidavit against him after hearing of his arrest; and based my affidavit against him upon what he said in the speech alluded to.

Question by Mr. Given—

What crime was Dr. Horton guilty of that you filed your affidavit against him?

Answer—He violated the proclamation of the President, discouraging enlistments, as I considered.

Question by Mr. Given—

Do you consider the proclamation of the President to which you refer the law of the land?

Answer—As Commander-in-Chief I consider that or any other proclamation to preserve, protect, and defend the Constitution and the integrity of the Republic in times of insurrection or rebellion, and during the existence of the same.

Question by Mr. Given—

Do you then consider that it is a crime to speak or argue against the views and policy of the Executive?

Answer—As a Civil Executive I do not; but as Commander-in-Chief I consider it both a crime and a burning shame for any person or persons to speak or act to impede the progress of our arms, to vindicate the rights of and support our Government, and put down a causeless and unholy rebellion.

Question by Mr. Given—

Can the President, by virtue of his office, exercise any except his civil authority over a State not in rebellion?

Answer—I believe he can when the public safety requires it.

A. B. JETMORE.

SIDNEY W. SEA (Posey County) SWORN.

Question by Mr. Baker—

Are you the Captain Sea referred to in the testimony of Baird and Mills in this investigation?

Answer—I am Captain in the Fifth Cavalry, stationed at Mount Vernon, Posey county, Indiana.

Question by Mr. Baker—

Do you know any thing about the arrest of Mills and Baird, and if so state it?

Answer—In regard to Baird's arrest, my suspicions had been directed to him some time before his arrest. He was known to be crossing the river repeatedly, and gone numbers of days at a time, ostensibly trading, but not trading in any thing openly except lately in coon skins, and it was supposed as there was goods gone from that point to guerrillas, that said Baird had some knowledge of their purchase and delivery. Baird is a man of notoriously bad character; he was in the habit of insulting the soldiers on the streets, stigmatizing them publicly as "d——d Lincoln puppies," and that any man that would fight in this army deserved hanging. This was what led to his arrest. On being arrested he was brought before me, and upon my questioning him as to his treatment of the soldiers, and his loyalty, he said that he could not support the war and would rot before he would take an oath to do it. I then ordered him to be placed outside of my tent, under the fly, on a good bed of straw, with blankets sufficient to keep him warm. He was disposed to be disorderly and noisy at first, but after he got quiet he remained still until morning, when I ordered a good horse for him to take him out of camp, when he concluded to take the oath, and as he said afterward, with the intention of keeping it.

Question by Mr. Baker—

Did Baird ask for any thing to eat, and did you refuse it?

Answer—He did not ask for any thing to eat that night, to my knowledge. We furnished him as good a breakfast in the morning as any of us had.

As to Mills, two of my men, while in his neighborhood, heard of his making disloyal remarks, and asked permission of me to visit him as citizens, which I granted. While at his house, they state that he said that he would be glad to see the cavalry up there all destroyed. They then told him that that was just what they came for; that they were a part of a band of guerrillas. He stated that he was glad to see them, and he would assist them all in his power. He said that a party of them could come to his house and remain; showed them where to put their horses if they came there in the night; and received from them a package or packages which they told him contained quinine and gun-caps, destined for the rebels. They say that he told them, and he don't deny it, that he would like to see Lincoln assassinated, and this cavalry blown to hell. This was what led to his arrest, together with other conversation of the same kind. I was at camp when he was brought there, but shortly left, and did not return until after he was released.

Question by Mr. Baker—

Who were the two soldiers who visited Mills' house?

Answer—Two cavalry men, named John S. Miller and Lafayette Finch.

Question by Mr. Baker—

Have you the affidavits of these two soldiers, stating the above facts, and, if so, can you produce them?

Answer—I have, I can, and now produce them in these words, to-wit:

Camp Graham, January 30, 1863.

John S. Miller and Lafayette Finch, being duly sworn, do depose and say, that having reason to suspect the loyalty of James S. Mills and John Bell, they proceeded to the house of said Mills, in disguise as Kentucky guerrillas, looking for a place to rendezvous, to secrete ammunition and contraband goods, and rest themselves and horses, telling said Mills that there was a large force of guerrillas ready to cross to take the Fifth Cavalry, (or that they were already across the river in force of 380 men,) and that they had four cannon, and wanted to fix the men in places as near the cavalry camp as possible. Mills was very much pleased to see the men in this character, and said Bell remarked that about half of the cavalry were Dutch, and did not amount to much, and he wished they were all in hell.

Bell further said, that most of the men in his neighborhood were all about right, and that when they came back they would know where to stop; but when they got to the plank-road they were mostly Abolitionists.

Mills said, then, that he would like to see old Lincoln's head taken off; cursed the Administration and the Lincoln Abolition war, and wanted to see this cavalry used up, if possible; was rejoiced the other detachments were taken, as reported, and recommended a certain place where to plant cannon so as to rake the tents with best effect.

Left with the understanding that they would return with a posse of men the same night; that he made arrangements where to put the horses and men.

And that said Miller and Finch did return this night, and requested said Mills to take care of and secrete a package, said to him to contain caps and quinine for the use of the rebels; the said Mills took them and put them away carefully, to produce at a moment's notice, after which I (Miller) called him out to assist in taking care of the horses of the guerrillas, (one of the horses was told him was captured from the Penn cavalry two days since). After his going out, they called Bell out, and arrested them both. They both showed a cheerful willingness to assist the guerrillas in every particular, and were anxious to do all in their power to defeat the cavalry, Abolitionists, and the Lincoln war.

Certified to before me, this 30th day of January, 1863.

SIDNEY W. SEA,
Captain, Commanding Camp Graham.

I will add that this last arrest was done more at the solicitation of the men, who have an impression that they should not rest under continual abuse by such men, and more for checking such treatment than for any punishment to this man particularly.

CROSS EXAMINATION.

Question by Mr. LASSELLE—

Were the above causes the only causes you had for the arrest of Baird and Mills?

Answer—That and general conduct tending to discourage soldiers and recruiting.

Question by Mr. LASSELLE—

Can you give any particular instance in which either Baird or Mills discouraged enlistments, of your own personal knowledge?

Answer—No, I can not; but have it from the best of authority.

Question by Mr. LASSELLE—

What is that authority?

Answer—It is that of numerous citizens and soldiers.

Question by Mr. LASSELLE—

Were any of them under oath at the time they made the statement?

Answer—None except the soldiers to whom I administered the oath.

Question by Mr. LASSELLE—

Who were the soldiers to whom you administered the oath?

Answer—I only remember the names of Finch and Miller.

Question by Mr. LASSELLE—

Were you authorized to administer oaths generally?

Answer—I am authorized to administer oaths to recruits, but I do not know whether I am authorized to administer oaths generally or not.

Question by Mr. LASSELLE—

Were these persons to whom you administered this oath recruits?

Answer—They were soldiers, already enlisted.

Question by Mr. LASSELLE—

Did you make these arrests upon your own or other authority?

Answer—Upon my own authority as commandant of the camp.

Question by Mr. GIVEN—

Do you know the place where the soldiers heard this conversation?

Answer—It was reported to me to have taken place at the house of this Mills, and in the town of Mount Vernon.

Question by Mr. GIVEN—

Who was the neighbor who you say invited the soldiers to visit them when they received the first information of the disloyalty of Mills?

Answer—I think it was a Mr. Allen.

Question by Mr. GIVEN—

State your opinion of Mills' mental capacity?

Answer—I should not think he had any superfluity of brains.

Question by Mr. GIVEN—

Are not all of the statements you have made as to the guilt of Baird and Mills, prior to their arrest, from hearsay and not from personal knowledge?

Answer—Principally by hearsay.

Question by Mr. GIVEN—

State where and when you heard either Baird or Mills say any thing that satisfied you of their disloyalty, and what was it?

Answer—Prior to their arrest, I can not locate any particular point, the time, or what they said.

Question by Mr. FERRIS—

Are you, or were you, at the time you administered the oath referred to above to Finch and Miller, holding any office whatever except that of Captain commanding camp and recruiting officer of the Fifth Indiana Cavalry.

Answer—I was not.

Question by Mr. Given—

In what do you consider treason to consist of?

Answer—I consider, at the present time, any thing that will hinder or demoralize the army, or place any obstacles in the way of its efficiency.

Question by Mr. Given—

Do you think treason can be committed by conversation?

Answer—I think there can be treasonable conversation.

SIDNEY W. SEA.

JONAS GOOD (Blackford County) SWORN.

Question by Mr. Baker—

State your name, age, residence and occupation?

Answer—My name is Jonas Good; aged thirty-one years; residence, Blackford county, and occupation a physician.

Question by Mr. Baker—

What do you know about the draft-box being destroyed at Hartford City?

Answer—I was in town on the day of the draft nearly all day. I was standing on the side-walk when I observed that there was going to be trouble. I heard Mr. Andrew B. Williams say, as he was passing by, that there would be no draft in town on that day. He said they (meaning the Abolitionists) were going to draft none but Democrats; he said that there would be fun by and bye; and went directly to the court house, where the arrangements were being made to proceed to draft. He appeared to be very much excited. This was in the fore part of the day, perhaps ten o'clock, or thereabouts. Shortly after I saw a crowd, perhaps twenty persons, assemble near the court house door, acting in a very boisterous manner, cursing and swearing, some of them with their sleeves rolled up, and hurrahing for Jeff. Davis. Those most conspicuous for their noise were Bluford Mills, John Daugherty, Thomas Daugherty, Jacob Clapper, Henry Snider, John Vanhorn, John Miller, and others whom I do not now remember. They then entered the court house. I entered shortly afterward. On entering the court house I saw twenty of twenty-five persons surrounding the officers connected with the drafting process. They were then acting in a very noisy manner, cursing and threatening the officers. The crowd was chiefly composed of those who had been assembled outside of the court house door. At this juncture I left the house, and crossed the street, when, within an hour or an hour and a-half, hearing a noise, I observed the crowd coming out of the court house in a very noisy manner, and some of them appeared to be rejoicing.

Cross Examination.

Question by Mr. Ferris—

How many men did you see at the court house door with their sleeves rolled up, and name them; and also state how far distant you was from them at the time?

Answer—I don't know how many. Jesse Williams, who was in the crowd, was one, but I can not name any others, with safety. I was about fifty yards off.

Question by Mr. Ferris—

If there was any other man boisterous in that crowd, than Williams, name him?

Answer—There was, but I can not name him.

Question by Mr. Ferris—

Did Bluford Mills, John Daugherty, Thomas Daugherty, Jacob Clapper, Henry Snider, John Vanhorn, John Miller, or either of them, have their sleeves rolled up?

Answer—I would not be certain, but I think so.

Question by Mr. Ferris—

Which one of these men do you "think" had his sleeves rolled up?

Answer—I can not dispose of that question.

Question by Mr. Ferris—

Are you positive that you know that one other man than Williams had his sleeves rolled up, and if so name him?

Answer—I am positive, though I can not name him.

Question by Mr. Ferris—

You say these men were cursing and swearing, what was that about?

Answer—The cursing and swearing I could distinctly hear. It

is my impression that they were enraged in consequence of the draft about to come off. I did hear some of them say some thing against the draft, but can not say who said it, or what it was. I obtain my impression from the boisterous manner of the crowd, and from their demonstrations.

Question by Mr. FERRIS—

What foundation had you for believing that the draft was to be resisted?

Answer—From what I heard Williams say, and the demonstrations of the crowd before the court house, and demonstrations generally.

Question by Mr. FERRIS—

Who else than Williams did you see in the court house with their sleeves rolled up, and name them if any?

Answer—I am satisfied that some of the same persons who assembled in front of the court house, and probably all of them who had their sleeves rolled up, outside of the house, were there.

Question by Mr. BROWN—

If you are satisfied that the same men whom you saw outside of the court house with their sleeves rolled up, were the same men you saw inside of the court house, why is it you can not name some others of them except Williams?

Answer—Williams was generally regarded as being a man of more fortitude and determination than some of the rest, consequently it was more natural to notice him more particularly than the rest.

Question by Mr. BROWN—

Are you acquainted with, and do you know, the names of all or any of the men you saw outside and inside of the court house?

Answer—I am partially acquainted with most of them, and know their names.

Question by Mr. BROWN—

If you are partially acquainted with these men, and know their names, why is it that you can not now give their names?

Answer—At the time I did not take down their names, consequently I do not now remember the names of persons, only those with whom I was most familiar.

Question by Mr. BROWN—

Do you know the names of the persons there who had their sleeves rolled up?

Answer—I knew their names at the time, but can not now call them.

Question by Mr. Brown—

Do you know their names now?

Answer—I do, but I can not call them.

Question by Mr. Brown—

Did you hear any person hallooing "hurrah for Jeff. Davis?"

Answer—I did.

Question by Mr. Brown—

Who were the persons?

Answer—Some of the crowd in front of the court house, but I can not give their names. I do not know their politics, for I do not know who hallooed.

Question by Mr. Brown—

What is your politics?

Answer—I have acted with the Republican party, but am now an unconditional Union man.

Question by Mr. Brown—

Did you file an affidavit against any of the persons who were arrested in your county, and if so, when?

Answer—I filed an affidavit against Williams, Bluford Mills, John Daugherty, Thomas Daugherty, Henry Snider, Jacob Clapper, Jesse Williams, and others, perhaps, whom I do not remember, after some of them had been arrested and taken away from Hartford.

Question by Mr. Brown—

How did you happen to make an affidavit against these men?

Answer—It was thought by the citizens generally that affidavits should be made against these men. I was notified by a person, whose name I do not now recollect, to appear before Justice Michael Cline, and I went there and made the affidavit.

Question by Mr. Brown—

Who were present at the magistrate's office at the time you made the affidavit?

Answer—A. B. Jetmore, Wm. A. Bonham, and some others, whom I do not recollect.

Question by Mr. Brown—

What is the politics of the men who were there—Democrat or Republican?

Answer—One of them, Jetmore, claims to be Union Democrat, I believe, and the other, Bonham, claims to be a Union man.

Question by Mr. Brown—

Was not Jetmore the Republican, or Union candidate for Representative of Blackford county, at the last election?

Answer—He was.

Question by Mr. Brown—

Was not the magistrate, at the time you made the affidavit, and is he not now, a Republican, or Unionist?

Answer—He claims to be a Unionist; acted with the Union party during the last canvas, I think, but was formerly a Douglas Democrat, and claims yet to be a Douglas Democrat.

Question by Mr. Brown—

Was there not a meeting of persons in your office, for the purpose of making affidavits against these men that were arrested?

Answer—There were several persons assembled at my office on the arrival of the soldiers, who, it was understood, came to enforce the draft, and among them were some of the military officers. They met there for the purpose of bringing to justice those whom it was understood had violated the laws of the country. Affidavits were then made against Brickley, John McManamon, Taughinbaugh, and others I do not now remember. I did not really know what would be the object of the meeting until they met there, though, of course, I had some idea.

Question by Mr. Brown—

Name the persons who met in your office at that time?

Answer—Colonel Tom. Browne was there, and did the writing, I believe; Wm. Frash, late Provost Marshal, and, I think, Goodin, the Commissioner, were there. Doctor Clowser was there, probably, and, perhaps, some others.

Question by Mr. Brown—

Are not all those whom you have named as being present at that meeting Unionists or Republicans?

Answer—They claim to be Unionists.

Question by Mr. Ferris—

Were not the two Williams' drunk at the time to which you refer in your testimony?

Answer—I think that they were under the influence, to some extent, of whisky.

JONAS GOOD.

WILLIAM A. BONHAM (Blackford County) SWORN.

Examined by Mr. Gregory—

My name is William A. Bonham; aged twenty-nine years; reside at Hartford City, Blackford county; occupation that of an attorney.

On the morning of the sixth of October last, I was in the clerk's office, when Sheriff Brickley came in. Soon after Andrew B. Williams also came in. Mr. Williams asked Mr. Brickley if he had any hand in the draft. Brickley answered No! It was the order that he was to place the ballots in the box, but they (meaning the Marshal and Commissioner), would not let him have any thing to do with it. Williams became very much enraged at the remark, and said he would shed the last drop of blood in his veins before he would be humbugged; said it was a d——d Abolition concern, and said it was managed by a set of black-hearted Abolitionists about that town. I afterward heard Williams repeat about the same on the street. I was in the court house about the time they commenced preparing the ballots. My attention was directed particularly to one Daniel Watson, who appeared to be very much excited—was talking loudly, and said the Enrolling Commissioner had stolen his name, and claimed that the draft was unfair on that account; said the Commissioner was not within ten miles of his residence. There were a good many persons in town that day. I noticed there was a dreadful feeling against the draft. Among those whom I noticed as being excited against the draft were A. B. Williams, Jesse Williams, Charles Williams, all brothers, John Daugherty, Thomas Daugherty, Daniel Watson, Bluford Mills, (since dead,) who said some week or two before the day of draft that he was armed to resist it, and knew of two hundred others who were the same.

I heard stamping and hallooing in the court house that day. After Bluford Mills was arrested, he said to me he would not have fled had he not been of the impression that they would hang or shoot him immediately; that he had laid in the swamps and it had had a very injurious effect on his health.

At this time I am an unconditional Union man. In 1856 I voted for Buchanan, but in 1860 I voted for Abraham Lincoln, and have been acting with that party since.

Question by Mr. Given—

Did you apprehend any trouble about the draft before the day upon which it occurred?

Answer—I did.

Question by Mr. GIVEN—

Did you make any effort on that day to prevent the trouble?

Answer—I did not; my reason for not interfering was that they were in the majority, and I did not think it safe.

Question by Mr. GIVEN—

Did you inform the sheriff of your county, or any other conservator of the peace, of your fears of trouble?

Answer—I did not. I advised the Commissioner to allow Sheriff Brickley to place the ballots in the box, or see it done.

Question by Mr. GIVEN—

What did you see Thomas Dougherty do?

Answer—I saw him with the crowd, and heard him swearing, but saw him commit no act of violence.

Question by Mr. GIVEN—

Were the crowd that you allude to on a "general bust," intoxicated, or were any of them so?

Answer—I think some of them were somewhat intoxicated.

Question by Mr. HOWARD—

How many persons were there in this crowd to which you allude?

Answer—I suppose fifteen or twenty.

Question by Mr. HOWARD—

What other evidence, beside their noisy and boisterous conduct, have you that these men, except the Williamses you have named, intended to destroy the draft-box?

Answer—The cursing and swearing is all, except what Harvey Snider said in my presence.

Question by Mr. GIVEN—

Did not this whole disturbance arise from the fact that Williams, who resided in another, was enrolled in the wrong township?

Answer—If that was the pretext, I was not aware of it from my personal knowledge.

Question by Mr. GIVEN—

Was it not the understanding that none but Democrats would be drafted?

Answer—I think not, among men who were informed.

Question by Mr. GIVEN—

Now do you not know that, by a preconcerted arrangement, none but Democrats were to be drafted?

Answer—I know there was not.

Examined by Mr. GIVEN—

You say you are an "unconditional Union man." Now if Mr. Lincoln should declare himself Dictator of this country, and, by so doing, restore the Union of these States, would you favor it?

(This question was protested against by Mr. Baker, Republican, for the reason that it had nothing to do with it.)

Answer—I refuse to answer.

Question by Mr. BAKER—

Who enrolled Jesse Williams?

Answer—I did, sir.

Question by Mr. BAKER—

Did he ever tell you he was enrolled in the wrong township?

Answer—He did not.

Question by Mr. BAKER—

Did you inform the Commissioner, or Provost Marshal, on the morning of the draft, that you apprehended danger?

Answer—I did.

W. A. BONHAM.

ALEXANDER DELONG (WELLS COUNTY) SWORN.

Question by Mr. BAKER—

State your name, age, residence and occupation?

Answer—My name is Alexander Delong; age fifty-seven years; reside at Wells county, Indiana; by occupation a farmer.

Question by Mr. BAKER—

Are you acquainted with Dr. Theodore Horton?

Answer—I am?

Question by Mr. BAKER—

Had you heard Dr. Horton, before his arrest, say any thing in opposition to the war or against enlistments?

Answer—I never heard him say any thing against enlistments; but have against the war.

Question by Mr. BAKER—

Please state what you heard him say against the war?

Answer—I heard him say that a Republican army could not be marched to the Ohio river before they would be stopped. I asked him who would stop them. He said the Democrats. I asked him if he would be in that army, and he said he would. I told him if I was on the other side I would shoot him, without orders. This was before the war broke out, and but a few days after Lincoln took his seat.

Question by Mr. BAKER—

Have you ever heard him make any other remarks about the war?

Answer—Yes; he said he was opposed to it.

Question by Mr. BROWN—

Did Dr. Horton give any reason for being opposed to the war, and if so, what was it?

Answer—He did: He said he was opposed to the suspension of the writ of *habeas corpus* and the Emancipation Proclamation; and that the war ought to be carried on without them.

Question by Mr. BROWN—

Did you ever hear him say at any other time that he would oppose the war, except the time when he stated that the Republican army could not march to the Ohio river?

Answer—I did not.

ALEXANDER DELONG.

WILLIAM A. CAMPBELL (BLACKFORD COUNTY) SWORN.

Examined by Mr. BAKER—

State your name, age, occupation, and place of residence?

Answer—My name is William A. Campbell; aged thirty-three years; and reside at Montpelier, Blackford county, Indiana.

Question by Mr. MORGAN—

Are you acquainted with William T. Schull, of Blackford county?

Answer—I am.

Question by Mr. MORGAN—

State what you heard him say, about the resistance to the draft, at Hartford City?

Answer—When he was informed, in my presence, of the mashing of the ballot-box, he said "good! good!" and that is what he was arrested for. Twible is the man who filed the affidavit against Schull.

Question by Mr. Ferris—

State particularly when, where, and in whose presence you heard Schull say this?

Answer—It was the evening of the 6th day of October, 1862, at Montpelier, in front of Boon & Twible's store, in the presence of Boon and Twible, and others.

Question by Mr. Ferris—

Do you positively swear that Twible, in his talk with Dr. Schull, stated where the draft-box was broken up?

Answer—Yes; he said, "your party, to-day, broke up the ballot-box at Hartford." The remark, and its answer, was made while Schull was passing on horseback. Schull did not stop on his way.

WM. A. CAMPBELL.

BENJAMIN S. NICKLIN (Wabash County) SWORN.

Examined by Mr. Morgan—

State your name, age, and present occupation?

Answer—My name is Benjamin S. Nicklin; aged thirty years; present occupation, a Captain in the Thirteenth Indiana Battery; residence, Wabash county, Indiana.

Question by Mr. Morgan—

State whether you made any arrests at Vevay, and the circumstances connected therewith?

Answer—I did arrest some of the citizens of Vevay, but do not remember the names of all of them, but remember the names of Clint McMahon, Dufour, and Kyle. I arrested them upon reliable information that they had been conveying information to the guerrilla bands across the river, on the Kentucky side. I derived the information from an army spy, of which I had many. I had no authority whatever, from Governor Morton, to make these arrests, and it was done without his knowledge.

Question by Mr. Ferris—

By whose authority, or by whose order, did you make these arrests?

Answer—By the general authority given to me by the military commanders at Louisville, to arrest all persons I had good reasons to suspect of disloyalty.

Question by Mr. Ferris—

Were the arrests made by you in Vevay, made solely upon the ground of hearsay testimony?

Answer—I made the arrests upon the statements of persons I did rely upon, but who were not under oath.

Question by Mr. Ferris—

Who was your informant upon whose statements you made these arrests?

Answer—I will not answer the question. Out of no disrespect to the Committee, however.

Question by Mr. Ferris—

Will you give the name of the person who gave you *the names* of the Vevay men who were arrested as Knights of the Golden Circle?

Answer—I decline to answer.

Question by Mr. Ferris—

You say that in making these arrests your men were armed, and that you ordered them to shoot down any man who made resistance. By what or whose authority did you give such orders?

Answer—I considered it my duty as an officer of the Army. Such are at all times my orders to my men when on duty.

Question by Mr. Morgan—

What is your politics?

Answer—I am a Democrat; always was a Democrat, and was a delegate to the 8th of January Convention, 1862.

Question by Mr. Morgan—

State why your men pointed their pistols at Mr. Kyle when they arrested him?

Answer—I was told that Mr. Kyle was attempting to escape; I ordered the men to follow him, and if he did not stop to shoot him. I have since learned that he made no attempt to escape.

BEN. S. NICKLIN.

JOHN PHIPPS (WELLS COUNTY) SWORN.

Question by Mr. MORGAN—

State your name, age, residence and occupation?

Answer—My name is John Phipps; aged thirty-three years; occupation that of a farmer; and reside in Wells county.

Question by Mr. MORGAN—

Are you acquainted with Dr. Theodore Horton?

Answer—I am.

Question by Mr. MORGAN—

State what you have ever heard him say, and what he has done in opposition to this war, and against the enlistment of soldiers?

Answer—At a war meeting held in the county of Wells, at Bare's school house, on or about the second of October last, when A. B. Jetmore, the Union candidate for Representative, and myself, arrived and made an effort to get volunteers. Near about the close of the meeting, Dr. Horton arrived, and said he had a few words to say. After ascending the rostrum he commenced as follows: Mr. Jetmore has been acting disgracefully to-night; illustrated it by an anecdote. He said it reminded him of the anecdote of a little boy who went out in company with other boys. One of the boys having killed a bird, this little fellow requested to have it—take possession of it. One who killed it proposed giving it to him if he would perform a disgraceful act, which he did. That the other boy refused giving the bird. He then went home crying. His mother asked him what was the matter, and he said one of his companions killed a bird, and offered to give it to him if he would disgrace himself. After doing so, he refused to give him the bird. Now, said he, Mr. Jetmore has disgraced himself before you to-night, to get the dead bird; but you won't give it to him fellow-citizens. This, said he, is an Abolition war. I always knew it to be an Abolition war; and now the President's proclamation has capped the Abolition climax. Here is a man here to-night (pointing to me) to get volunteers. You are not going to volunteer in a war carried on under any such policy. No, not one of you. He then gave his definition of Abolitionists, saying that the Abolitionists are those now in power, and all that sustain the Administration were Abolitionists. These Abolitionists must be removed from power by the dropping of little bits of paper into the ballot-box, and Democrats put into their place. Then we will arm ourselves and shoot down these Abolitionists. That is the war you will fight in fellow-citizens, aint it? That is about the amount of his remarks. I never heard him express himself upon the subject at any other time.

Question by Mr. MORGAN—

Was this meeting called for the purpose of getting volunteers?

Answer—Mr. Jetmore, as the Union candidate for Representative for that District, had given public announcement that he would make a "Union" speech on that occasion; and as I was acting in the capacity of a recruiting officer for the Thirty-fourth Regiment Indiana Volunteers, and would have to canvass the county; that if I would have bills struck announcing war meetings at the same time and place with his appointments, after making his "Union" speech he would give me and Mr. Banta, a man who was to address those war meetings, all the assistance he could in the way of speaking to get volunteers. That meeting was announced according to this arrangement. These are all the facts I know in connection with this matter.

CROSS EXAMINATION.

Question by Mr. LASSELLE—

Did you not file an affidavit, and cause Dr. Horton to be arrested for making the statements as above represented by you?

Answer—I filed an affidavit setting forth the language of Dr. Horton at that meeting, believing his language came within the perview of the President's proclamation, in reference to discouraging enlistments.

Question by Mr. LASSELLE—

What are Dr. Horton's political sentiments?

Answer—I have always understood he was a Democrat.

Question by Mr. LASSELLE—

What are your political sentiments?

Answer—I vote the "Union" ticket.

Question by Mr. LASSELLE—

What did you do with your affidavit against Dr. Horton?

Answer—I left it in the possession of Dwight Klinck to be sent to Indianapolis. I inquired for the proper person to be sent to, and Klinck informed me that it should be sent to Colonel Rose, United States Marshal, at Indianapolis; and that he would send it.

Question by Mr. LASSELLE—

State whether if the political discussion you refer to between Dr.

Horton and A. B. Jetmore had not been called by Jetmore publicly by hand-bills as a political meeting?

Answer—I do not know.

Question by Mr. Lasselle—

Did Jetmore not call the meeting by hand-bills as a Union meeting?

Answer—He called it as a meeting where he designed making a Union speech.

Question by Mr. Lasselle—

Was not your so-called "Union party" a political party?

Answer—Yes; I suppose it was.

Question by Mr. Brown—

Did not Mr. Jetmore, at that meeting, discuss political questions, and urge his claims for election to the Indiana Legislature?

Answer—He discussed the issues that were before the people, and urged his claims for election to the Legislature in the first part of his speech, and the latter part was an appeal for the people to volunteer.

Question by Mr. Lasselle—

State if it was not after Jetmore was entirely through with his address, that Dr. Horton, upon the invitation of part of the meeting, made his speech in reply to the political part of Jetmore's address?

Answer—I do not know whether or not he was invited to speak; but he was not called upon audibly in the meeting; and he did not commence to speak until Jetmore was through.

Question by Mr. Lasselle—

Was not the anecdote represented by you as having been related by Dr. Horton at that meeting, so related by him to illustrate the position of Jetmore, as having left the Democratic party and joined the Abolition party, under the promise of being elected Representative?

Answer—I did not think so in connection with his speech at the time.

Question by Mr. Lasselle—

Was it not true that Jetmore had recently left the Democratic party and joined what you term the Union party, and then a candidate of that party for Representative?

Answer—I heard Mr. Jetmore say he had formerly been a member of the Democratic party; and he was then a candidate for Representative on the Union ticket.

Question by Mr. HANNA—

State whether you are personally acquainted with Dwight Klinck, and how long have you known him?

Answer—I am, and have known him for the last five or six months.

Question by Mr. HANNA—

State what his political sentiments were during the last October election, on the issues then dividing the Democratic and Republican parties.

Answer—He was the "Union" candidate for Senator.

Question by Mr. HANNA—

Am I to understand that you state that at the time you delivered your affidavit against Dr. Horton to him to be sent to the United States Marshal, that he was the Republican candidate for State Senator?

Answer—Yes, he was the candidate at that time.

Question by Mr. BROWN—

Did you not come to this city for the purpose of being examined as a witness before the United States Grand Jury?

Answer—I did, in obedience to a summons served upon me by the sheriff of my county.

Question by Mr. MORGAN—

State whether you made any effort to get volunteers at that meeting referred to in your affidavit; in what way, and what occurred afterwards?

Answer—When Mr. Jetmore had concluded his appeal to the people to volunteer, I stated that I was there to get recruits, and would take the descriptive rolls after the speeches should be concluded. As I took my seat, Dr. Horton rose up and said: "I have a few words to say ——," and made the speech I have already related.

Question by Mr. BROWN—

Did you not state—when you stated you was prepared to enlist volunteers—that you would enlist volunteers after the speaking had closed; and was it not immediately after you had so spoken that Dr. Horton began to make his speech, and did you not think it improper for you to attempt to enlist volunteers between speaking?

Answer—I did say that I would make out the enlistment rolls of any that might desire to volunteer at the close of the speeches, and Horton began speaking as soon as I had made that statement.

I thought that if Jetmore's competitor, who was present, desired to reply, it would be no more than fair to wait until he had spoken. I had no expectation or knowledge that Horton intended to speak.

JOHN PHIPPS.

WILLIAM FRASH (Blackford County) SWORN.

General question in chief by Mr. Baker—

Answer—My name is William Frash; aged fifty-four years; by occupation a merchant; reside at Hartford City, in Blackford county.

Question by Mr. Baker—

Do you know any thing about the draft-box being mashed at Hartford City, on or about the 6th of October last, and, if so, state it?

Answer—I saw the box destroyed, together with the ballots which were in it. I was Provost Marshal, and, as it was my duty, I was in the court house about one o'clock, in company with Goodin, in charge of the draft-box. We had placed three ballots in the box when Peter Kamer, who had been selected by the Commissioner to draw the ballots, refused to serve, and Sheriff Brickley remarked, that if he could not act by authority he would have nothing to do with it. A rumor had gained currency that it was the sheriff's place to do the drawing; but I explained that it was my place to do so, and voices cried out, "let the right one do it." Before this, Sheriff Brickley had agreed with myself and the Commissioner and Kamer to stand by and see the drafting fairly done. After the three ballots were placed in the box he refused to have any thing further to do with it, unless he could do it officially, and then Kamer refused. I then asked Brickley who was the proper one to do it—me or him. He answered, that he was. I replied, "I think I am, and I am going to make the draft." Brickley then left, and I did not see him afterward as I recollect of. In fifteen or twenty minutes afterward, Jesse Williams came in and broke the box by mashing it on the floor and stamping it. Whereupon a general hurrah and hallooing commenced in the court house. Williams, after breaking the box, attempted to strike at me with a club, and was prevented (as I was informed) by Chris. Clapper, who held his arm. Michael Daugherty, at this time, stood in front of Williams and forbade his striking me, holding a cane up to protect me, when Frank. Taughinbaugh pushed Daugherty's cane out of the way. At this moment John Diskey whispered to me that I was in danger, and advised me to leave. When I was gathering up the enrollment lists Williams snatched one of them and started out of the house, the greater part of the crowd following him. I found I could do nothing and went home.

Question by Mr. Baker—

How many persons were there in the house at the time the box was mashed?

Answer—I should think forty or fifty.

Question by Mr. Baker—

Give the names of those who were present.

Answer—Abraham Stahl, Madison Garret, Leander Tarr, Chris. Clapper, Allen Ward, William Gabel, and others I do not remember.

Question by Mr. Baker—

Why did you ask Brickley to stand by and see the thing fairly done?

Answer—Because Brickley and Kamer were identified as Democrats, and in order to satisfy their party. Kamer was to draw the tickets and Brickley to see it done.

Question by Mr. Gregory—

Did you hear any one speak of resisting the draft in the forenoon of that day?

Answer—John Diskey said there would be no draft that day; and one of the Williams' said the same.

Cross Examination.

Question by Mr. Shoaff—

What did Williams say when he mashed the box?

Answer—I don't know any thing; only he cursed and swore.

Question by Mr. Shoaff—

Did you consider him intoxicated or not?

Answer—I considered him intoxicated.

Question by Mr. Shoaff—

Did any one, beside Williams, to your knowledge, interfere to break the draft-box; and, if so, who were they?

Answer—Williams alone broke the box, and immediately after it was broken others kicked the pieces of the box with a general hurrah among them.

Question by Mr. SHOAFF—

Was there any Republican or Union men in the court house at the time?

Answer—There was some there, but I only recognized two.

Question by Mr. SHOAFF—

Are you sure that the hurrahing was done exclusively by Democrats?

Answer—You may have it so.

Question by Mr. GREGORY—

What is your politics?

Answer—I always was a Democrat, and acted with that party ever since I had a vote; and voted for Douglas.

Question by Mr. SHOAFF—

Did you vote the Republican, or so-called Union ticket, at the last election?

Answer—I voted the Union ticket throughout.

W. FRASH.

CHRISTOPHER CLAPPER (BLACKFORD COUNTY) SWORN.

General question in chief by Mr. BAKER—

My name is Christopher Clapper; aged thirty years; residence Blackford county, Indiana.

Question by Mr. BAKER—

Do you know any thing about the draft-box being destroyed at Hartford City, on or about the sixth of October last; and, if so, state what you know about it?

Answer—I was in the room when the box was broken. There was some excitement in the house; Brickley, the sheriff, claiming that he had the right to do the drafting. Brickley had told me that morning, before they went in to draft, that unless he could act as an officer according to the first order, he would have nothing to do with it; and just before we entered the room Mr. Kamer informed me that he and Brickley had agreed that they were to assist each other; and were there about the time the tickets were to be put in. Brickley left the stand first, and was followed soon after by Kamer. Then Goodin (Commissioner) passed around the crowd hunting some one to occupy that post, when he was met by Andy Williams, who said to him, "If you undertake to draft a man here to-day, we will take you out and not leave an inch of your body." Shortly after I saw the box go up above the people's heads. I did not see who done it; but as it struck the floor I saw Jesse Williams jump on it, and stamp it; at which time there was cheering and hallooing in the house. Jesse Williams then seized one of the legs of the drafting machine, and was in the act of striking William Frash, when I caught his arm. Jesse Williams then snatched one of the enrollment lists, and started for the door with it in his hand. Shortly after he went out of the room—the crowd left the house. I left, then, for home, a few minutes afterward.

Question by Mr. Baker—

State the names of all those you remember being present at the time the draft-box was broken, beside those you have mentioned?

Answer—Peter Kamer (nephew of the Kamer I have named) and Allen Ward. I cannot positively state as to the names of any others being present at that time.

Question by Mr. Baker—

Give the names of all those who you remember being there in the crowd, during the time they were preparing to draft?

Answer—Beside all those I have already mentioned, John Daugherty, Thomas Daugherty, and another Daugherty, John McManamon, Franklin M. Taughinbaugh, Jacob Clapper, Henry Snider, William Clapper, Henry Huffman, and John Diskey.

Question by Mr. Baker—

Did the crowd, or any part of it, in the court house, at the time the box was destroyed, seem to uphold Williams in destroying the box?

Answer—There were cheers in various parts of the house, hurrahing for Jeff. Davis and the Southern Confederacy, but I am not able to state who done it.

Question by Mr. Baker—

What is your politics?

Answer—I have voted the Democratic ticket; and voted that ticket at the last election.

Question by Mr. Ferris—

Were there quite a number of Republicans present in the house when the draft-box was broken?

Answer—There were some present.

Question by Mr. Ferris—

Now, can you state positively, whether it was the Democrats or Republicans who were hallooing?

Answer—I can not. With the exception of Williams, I can not tell whether they were Democrats or Republicans.

Question by Mr. Ferris—

Was there any active demonstrations, in opposition to the draft, made by any one present except the two Williams'?

Answer—There was not.

Question by Mr. Ferris—

What do you know in regard to the impression among the Democrats there, that none but Democrats were to be drafted in that county; and what did you hear Republicans say in regard to the matter?

Objected to by Mr. Morgan.

Answer—I heard several Democrats say they (meaning the Republicans) intended to draft all Democrats. I heard no Republicans say any thing of the sort.

Question by Mr. Ferris—

Did Frash, the Provost Marshal, or Goodin, the Commissioner, at or before the disturbance, make any effort whatever to preserve order or enforce the draft, or call upon the bystanders to protect them in the performance of their duties?

Answer—One of the three—Frash, Brickley or Goodin—called for "order," some ten or fifteen minutes before the box was mashed, and it is my impression that Brickley made the call. I heard no further call.

CHRISTOPHER CLAPPER.

DWIGHT KLINCK (Wells County) SWORN.

General question in chief by Mr. Morgan—

Answer—My name is Dwight Klinck; aged twenty-seven years; reside at Bluffton, Wells county; and am at present engaged in the Banking business; have resided in Wells county about two years and three months.

Question by Mr. Morgan—

Are you acquainted with John Phipps, and, if so, how long have you been acquainted with him?

Answer—I have been acquainted with him about one year.

Question by Mr. Morgan—

Are you acquainted with his general character?

Answer—I am.

Question by Mr. Morgan—

Is it good or bad?

Answer—It is good.

Cross Examination.

Question by Mr. Lasselle—

How far do you live from Mr. Phipps?

Answer—About two miles.

Question by Mr. Lasselle—

Have you taken any pains to inquire as to his character?

Answer—I have sir; considerable.

Question by Mr. Lasselle—

When did you make these inquiries?

Answer—Since his character came in question on account of Phipps' affidavit against Dr. Horton.

Question by Mr. Lasselle—

In what neighborhood did that question as to the character of Mr. Phipps arise?

Answer—In Bluffton and vicinity.

Question by Mr. Lasselle—

Did you not confine these inquiries to the political friends of Mr. Phipps and yourself?

Answer—I think I did not.

Question by Mr. Lasselle—

Can you name any persons not belonging to your party, of whom you made such inquiry?

Answer—I could not particularly, as my inquiry was general.

Question by Mr. LASSELLE—

State if you have not heard in the neighborhood of Phipps, that he had been charged or convicted of perjury?

Answer—Mr. Phipps told me himself that at Vicksburgh, Miss., he was charged with perjury, and duly acquitted.

Question by Mr. LASSELLE—

Did Phipps make his affidavit against Horton before you, and if so, what did he do with it?

Answer—He made the affidavit before me as Notary Public, and I left it in his hands.

Question by Mr. LASSELLE—

Did you or did you not at any time retain that affidavit in your hands?

Answer—I left it in the possession of Phipps and T. W. Wilson. It was in Wilson's office that I wrote it. I don't know which one took it.

Question by Mr. LASSELLE—

Did you not at the time tell Phipps that you would retain the affidavit and have it sent to Marshal Rose?

Answer—I am quite sure I did not.

DWIGHT KLINCK.

JAMES CROSBIE (WELLS COUNTY) SWORN.

General Question in chief by Mr. MORGAN—

Answer—My name is James Crosbie; aged forty-two years; occupation a farmer, and reside in Wells county, Indiana.

Question by Mr. MORGAN—

Do you know John Phipps, and are you acquainted with his general moral character?

Answer—I am not much acquainted with him personally. I have known him personally since the first of October last. He has a good moral character so far as I know.

Question by Mr. BAKER—

Are you acquainted with Dr. Horton?

Answer—Yes sir.

Question by Mr. BAKER—

Had you ever heard him say any thing in opposition to the war or against enlistments prior to his arrest?

Answer—Yes; I heard him make a speech in Nottingham township, Wells county, on the evening of October the second, 1862, in which he said, "Mr. Phipps has asked you to volunteer. Did he get any? No, not one. You was not going to volunteer under such a policy. I always knew that this was an Abolition war; and since the Proclamation of the President it has topped it with the Abolition climax. He then proceeded to reply to the speech of Jetmore, defending Voorhees' speech, said where is the Democrat but what would do the same thing—stand up between the tax payer and the tax gatherer. You are earning your money by the sweat of your brow, and they are stealing it from you." Dr. Horton did not rise to address this meeting until after the conclusion of Jetmore's speech and the appeal of Phipps for volunteers was over. He passed to the stand to speak, from one to three minutes after Phipps had concluded, and no volunteers offered. In the speech of Horton, I will add, he also said (holding a paper in his hand wrapped up as a ballot) we will kill off the Abolitionists with these (meaning the ballots), reinstate the Democratic party, and go South and shoot down the Rebels with bullets.

Cross Examination.

Question by Mr. Shoaff—

Did Dr. Horton, in the speech you allude to, denounce the policy of the war, or the war itself?

Answer—So far as I understood him, it was the *policy* of the war.

JAMES CROSBIE.

ABRAHAM STAHL (Blackford County) SWORN.

General question in chief by Mr. Morgan—

My name is Abraham Stahl; aged fifty-three years; occupation a farmer; and reside in Blackford county, Indiana.

Question by Mr. Morgan—

State what you know about the draft-box being mashed, at Hartford City, and who participated in it?

Answer—On the sixth of October, the day of the attempted draft, I was in the court house. While they were making preparations a dispute arose between Sheriff Brickley and Frash, Provost Marshall, as to which of them should place the tickets in the box. During the dispute, Brickley asked Frash which had the right to place the tickets in the box, and Frash answered that *he* had the right—that Stanton's order was superceded by that of Governor Morton. Brickley then left the stand, having said that he would have nothing more to do with it. When the box was mashed I heard the crash, but did not see who done it. When the box was mashed there was hallooing and cheering in the house. I saw Jesse Williams with a piece of the box in his hands. I can not designate the persons who hallooed and cheered.

Question by Mr. Ferris—

Did you see any body making demonstrations there except the Williams'?

Answer—I did not.

ABRAHAM STAHL.

ALLEN WARD (Blackford County) SWORN.

General question in chief by Mr. Morgan—

My name is Allen Ward; aged thirty-six years; reside in Blackford county; and by occupation a farmer.

Question by Mr. Morgan—

State what you know about resisting and mashing the draft-box at Hartford City?

Answer—I was present at the time the preparations for the draft were being made. When the draft-box was brought in the question arose as who should do the drafting, Brickley contending that he had the right to do it under the first order, and Provost Marshal Frash claiming that he should do it. Brickley was willing to go on with it under the first order. On the second order Frash claimed it. Brickley then refused to do it on them terms. After two or three of the tickets were put in John Daugherty kicked the box over; then Jesse Williams kicked it two or three times, and then gathered it and threw it up to the ceiling. After it fell down they jumped on it, and stamped it all to pieces. Then Jesse Williams drew a leg off the frame and attempted to strike Frash. when Christopher Clapper caught his arm. After the box was torn to pieces they commenced their hallooing.

Question by Mr. MORGAN—

Who did you see engaged in stamping on the box?

Answer—I saw Jesse Williams, Andrew Williams, John Daugherty, Thomas Daugherty, John Vanhorn, and Bluford Mills.

Question by Mr. MORGAN—

Who did you see hallooing, cheering and stamping on the floor?

Answer—Besides these I have named, I saw Leander Tarr, Daniel Watson, Huey Lyons, John Miller, Henry Snider, and John P. Garr.

CROSS EXAMINATION.

Question by Mr. FERRIS—

What is your politics?

Answer—I am a Republican.

Question by Mr. FERRIS—

How many men were there in the court house when the draft-box was mashed?

Answer—About a hundred.

Question by Mr. FERRIS—

Do you swear positively that Jesse Williams, Andrew Williams, John and Thomas Daugherty, John Vanhorne, and Bluford Mills, were each of them engaged in stamping the box and throwing the pieces around?

Answer—Yes, sir.

uestion by Mr. FERRIS—

ow much was the box broken; into how many pieces?

swer—The rim was broken into two pieces, and each head into the same number of pieces—I am positive.

Question by Mr. FERRIS—

Who did you see throwing the pieces around?

Answer—I can not name any person.

Question by Mr. FERRIS—

Name the person you know you saw stamping the box?

Answer—I saw Jess. Williams. He is the only one I can swear I saw stamping the box.

Question by Mr. Ferris—

If you stated that any person except Williams stamped on the box or the pieces, was that true?

Answer—To be certain, Jess. Williams was the only person I saw stamping the box or the pieces.

Question by Mr. Ferris—

Could you have heard it, had any one hurrahed for Jeff. Davis before the crowd left the court house?

Answer—Yes, I could.

Question by Mr. Ferris—

Was there any hallooing for Jeff. Davis in the house?

Answer—If there was I did not hear it.

Question by Mr. Ferris—

If you swore that any of the six men you named besides Williams was engaged in throwing around the pieces of the box, was that statement true?

Answer—I saw none but Williams have hold of the box or any of the pieces.

Question by Mr. Ferris—

If you stated that Leander Tarr, Daniel Watson, Henry Snider, John P. Garr, and John Miller were there hallooing, was that statement true?

Answer—I can not be positive that every one of them was.

Question by Mr. Ferris—

Was there any stamping done in the room that you know of except that done on the box?

Answer—None that I could name.

Question by Mr. Ferris—

Now if you stated that any person except Williams was engaged in stamping on the floor, was that statement true?

Answer—I saw John Doherty and Bluford Mills jumping up and down on the floor.

Question by Mr. Ferris—

Do you state positively that any one present in the court house really hallooed but John Doherty and Bluford Mills?

Answer—Not to be positive, I could not.

ALLEN WARD.

INDEX.

A

B

C

D

F

G

H

J

K

L

M

N

P

R

S

T

V

W

Z

www.ingramcontent.com/pod-product-compliance
Lightning Source LLC
LaVergne TN
LVHW021359110826
845150LV00007B/1710